I0446254

SHAH MOHAMMED

Innovation's Hidden Walls

Uncovering Limitations of Jobs To Be Done, Design Thinking, and the Diffusion of Innovation Model.

Copyright © 2023 by Shah Mohammed

All rights reserved. No part of this publication may be reproduced, stored or transmitted in any form or by any means, electronic, mechanical, photocopying, recording, scanning, or otherwise without written permission from the publisher. It is illegal to copy this book, post it to a website, or distribute it by any other means without permission.

First edition

This book was professionally typeset on Reedsy.
Find out more at reedsy.com

Contents

Introduction		iv
1	Limitations of Jobs to be Done	1
2	Limitations of Design Thinking	45
3	Limitations of the Diffusion of Innovation Model	86
4	Challenges of Group Brainstorming	158
About the Author		164
Also by Shah Mohammed		166

Introduction

In a world that continually demands innovation and progress, the pathways to creative problem-solving have become more diverse than ever before. Concepts like Jobs To Be Done, Design Thinking, and the Diffusion of Innovation model have emerged as powerful tools for individuals, businesses, and industries seeking to navigate the complex landscape of invention and change. These methods offer structured approaches to understanding customer needs, generating new ideas, and ensuring widespread adoption of innovations. They are hailed as the gold standards of modern business strategy, celebrated for their potential to revolutionize the way we create and introduce new products and services.

However, beyond the shining promises and celebrated successes, there exists a hidden truth — the limitations and boundaries that these methodologies may impose. These constraints often remain concealed behind the allure of innovative thinking, waiting to be unearthed and explored. In "Innovation's Hidden Walls: Uncovering Limitations of Jobs To Be Done, Design Thinking, and the Diffusion of Innovation Model," we embark on a compelling journey to illuminate these barriers.

This book is a critical exploration of the hidden walls that restrict our understanding and application of Jobs To Be Done, Design Thinking, and the Diffusion of Innovation model. Through an in-depth examination, we shed light on the misconceptions, biases, cultural variations, and other factors that can sabotage our pursuit of innovation. These limitations challenge the very foundations of these methodologies, reshaping our perspective on how we innovate and bring change into the world.

We delve into the central themes of each methodology, critically analyzing the underlying assumptions, shedding light on the biases that lie beneath the surface, and exposing the inconsistencies that may lead us astray. We explore how cultural and contextual variations can influence the impact of these methodologies, highlighting that they are not universally applicable across all regions and communities. Our journey takes us deep into the human psyche, revealing the role of emotions, biases, and cognitive tendencies that may defy conventional problem-solving approaches. We also confront the influence of external events and social dynamics that disrupt the well-structured models we hold dear.

"Innovation's Hidden Walls" serves as a navigational guide for innovators, entrepreneurs, designers, and strategic thinkers. It encourages us to reevaluate the way we approach problems and challenges the established conventions of innovation. While acknowledging the significance of Jobs To Be Done, Design Thinking, and the Diffusion of Innovation model, we go beyond their perceived boundaries to decipher a more comprehensive perspective.

In the chapters that follow, we uncover the secrets behind these limitations, exploring how businesses and individuals can break free from these hidden walls to unlock their full potential for innovation. We reveal that innovation is not confined to the methodologies themselves but resides in the human capacity to adapt, evolve, and transcend the established norms.

Join us on this enlightening journey as we dismantle the concealed boundaries of innovation and step into a world where innovation knows no walls.

* * *

1

Limitations of Jobs to be Done

The Jobs to be Done (JTBD) framework has gained popularity as a valuable tool for businesses to understand their customers better. Developed by Clayton Christensen, a professor at Harvard Business School, the JTBD framework shifts the focus from merely looking at customer preferences or demographics to understanding customers' underlying needs and motivations.

The core idea of the JTBD framework is that customers do not purchase products or services solely for the sake of having them; instead, they seek to fulfil a particular job or task they need to accomplish in a particular context. This job can be a specific task or a broader goal. By identifying the specific job customers are trying to achieve and comprehending its context and circumstances, businesses can gain deeper insights into their customers' needs and desires.

Rather than getting fixated on the features or benefits of a product, the JTBD framework encourages businesses to concentrate on the job the product or service is intended to help customers accomplish more effectively. This approach enables businesses to develop products and services that align better with what customers truly want, leading to more effective solutions and stronger customer relationships.

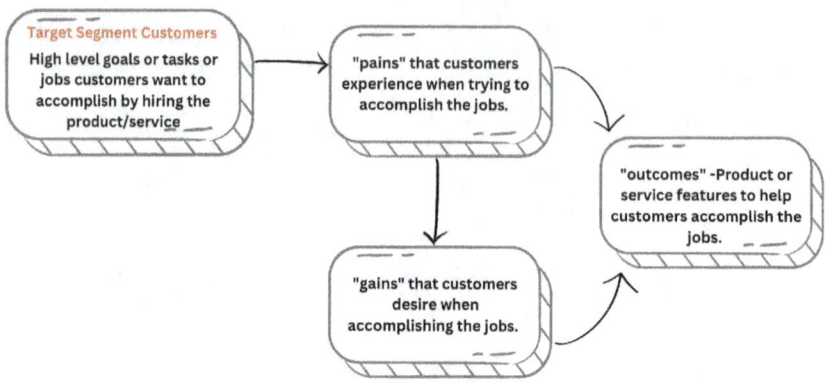

A brief visual representation of the Jobs to be Done (JTBD) framework.

Let's consider an example of a coffee shop chain that applies the Jobs to be Done (JTBD) framework to understand its customers and enhance its product offerings.

In the highly competitive coffee shop industry, a coffee shop chain seeks to gain a competitive edge by understanding its customers better and enhancing its offerings. To achieve this, the company adopts the Jobs to be Done (JTBD) framework, which shifts the focus from simply selling products to comprehending customers' underlying needs and motivations.

Rather than considering customers merely seeking a cup of coffee, the coffee shop chain recognizes that customers are attempting different jobs when they visit. These jobs range from seeking a quick energy boost in the morning before work to desiring a cozy environment for socializing with friends or colleagues in the evenings. Some customers may visit the coffee shop to find a comfortable spot to work or study, while others see it as a refreshing break during a busy shopping trip.

With a deeper understanding of the context and circumstances surrounding each job, the coffee shop chain tailors its offerings accordingly. The company introduces a specialized express lane for morning commuters to ensure quick and efficient service during busy hours. Recognizing the preferences of socializing customers, the coffee shop creates larger seating areas with comfortable couches and group tables to foster a welcoming atmosphere.

To accommodate those seeking a work or study space, the coffee shop offers free Wi-Fi and designated quiet zones to create a conducive environment for productivity. For shoppers on a break, the company strategically opens new locations within shopping malls and commercial areas for their convenience.

By aligning its products and services with the specific jobs customers are trying to accomplish, the coffee shop chain succeeds in becoming more customer-centric. This approach enhances customer satisfaction, fosters loyalty, and encourages positive word-of-mouth within the community. As a result, the chain not only retains existing customers but also attracts new ones, propelling its growth and success in the competitive market.

JBTD(Sample) -A Coffee Chain

Morning Office Commuters
Seeking a quick energy boost in the morning before work.

Pains
Could not order quickly, waiting for delivery, spillage from cups while travelling

Outcomes
Self-order Kiosks(swipe and take delivery), pre-prepared beverages, Express lanes.

Gains
Customers desire a quick, efficient, convenient ordering process. Quick delivery. Sealed Cups

Let's consider another example of a fitness equipment company that adopts the Jobs to be Done (JTBD) framework.

In the ever-evolving fitness industry, a fitness equipment company strives to stand out by better understanding its customers and refining its product offerings. Realizing that customers don't simply buy fitness products for the sake of having equipment, the company adopts the Jobs to be Done (JTBD) framework to gain deeper insights into the underlying needs and motivations of its customers.

Through the JTBD framework, the company identifies the specific jobs that customers want to achieve through fitness equipment. These jobs include achieving personal fitness goals, seeking convenience and time efficiency in their workouts, desiring enjoyable and engaging exercise experiences, and wanting to track their progress and performance over time.

To delve further into the context and circumstances surrounding each job, the fitness equipment company conducts thorough research. This reveals that customers with different fitness goals require various types of equipment, such as treadmills for cardio, weights for strength training, or yoga mats for flexibility exercises. Additionally, time-crunched individuals prefer space-saving and multifunctional equipment that can be easily incorporated into their daily routines. Customers also value interactive features, virtual training programs, and user-friendly interfaces that provide real-time data on their workouts' intensity and progress.

Armed with these valuable insights, the fitness equipment company tailors its product offerings to cater to the diverse needs of its customers. It offers a wide range of equipment, from cardio machines to strength training tools, ensuring customers find the right equipment to support their unique fitness objectives. The company focuses on creating space-saving and foldable options for those seeking convenience and time efficiency. To make workouts enjoyable and engaging, interactive displays, virtual training programs, and workout challenges are incorporated into the equipment. The company also integrates advanced fitness tracking technology to allow users to monitor their progress and set personalized goals.

By aligning its products with the underlying jobs that customers aim to accomplish, the fitness equipment company fosters a customer-centric approach that elevates the overall fitness experience. As a result, customers experience higher satisfaction, leading to increased loyalty and positive word-of-mouth. The company's reputation as a trusted fitness equipment provider grows, enabling it to thrive in the competitive market.

* * *

Limitations of the JTBD Framework

While the JTBD framework has proven to be a valuable tool for businesses, it's important to recognize its limitations. Understanding these limitations is critical for companies looking to make informed decisions about product development and marketing strategies.

01 Identity-based Needs

In the world of consumer preferences, there is a fascinating interplay between the functional aspects of a product and the emotional and aspirational needs it fulfils. Take, for example, the simple act of purchasing a car. Functionally, all cars serve the same purpose of transporting us from point A to point B. Yet, when it comes to buying a car, we often find ourselves drawn to specific brands for reasons beyond mere functionality. Cars become coveted status symbols, whether we consciously admit it or not.

To illustrate this phenomenon, a focus group was asked, "What would your friends think of you if they saw you driving this new car?" The initial response was an air of subtle arrogance, with participants asserting that they didn't care about others' opinions; they just wanted reliable transportation.

However, when presented with various car concepts and asked about their preferred choices, the same group members gravitated towards vehicles with "head-turning" looks. It became evident that, deep down, everyone desires recognition and attention from others. The car they choose becomes an extension of their identity, a way to project a certain image to the world.

This aspect of identity-based needs is one limitation of the Jobs to be Done (JTBD) framework. While JTBD is effective in understanding customers' functional needs and motivations, it may fall short in capturing the emotional and aspirational needs that strongly influence consumer behaviour.

The popularity of athletic wear and workout clothes serves as another compelling example. Today, it's not just about creating functional apparel for exercise; it's about crafting an identity that customers want to advertise. Millennials, in particular, unconsciously showcase their fitness attitude and healthy lifestyle to the outside world. They desire recognition within their community, potential mates, and the acquisition of power.

Recognizing this, brands have launched fashionable workout clothes that are so appealing that people wear them outside the gym. These high-performance fabrics come at a premium, yet individuals gladly invest in them as they enable them to broadcast their fitness identity and healthy lifestyle status.

Celebrity endorsement is another powerful tool brands use to sell an identity to customers. This appeals to the desire to emulate the athlete or celebrity they idolize, as it reflects the customer's aspiration to be just like their role model.

In the realm of luxury cars, customers may choose a particular brand not solely for transportation purposes but because it aligns with their identity and values. The car brand becomes a symbol of their status, success, and taste, making it an integral part of their self-identity.

Similarly, high-end fashion products are not merely chosen for their functional features but also for the emotional and aspirational benefits they offer, such as confidence, attractiveness, and sophistication.

Brands that can tap into customers' identity-based needs create powerful emotional connections, leading to loyalty and repeat purchases. JTBD, with its focus on functional needs, may not fully capture these deeper aspects of consumer behaviour.

02 Creating New Needs

While JTBD can be a useful tool for understanding customers' current needs and motivations, it may not be effective in predicting or creating new needs and behaviours.

Nike—In the late 1960s, jogging was far from being a popular activity, and those who attempted it faced skepticism and hostility from onlookers who threw beer and soda cans at them. However, two visionaries, Bill Bowerman and Phil Knight, saw the potential for jogging to promote a healthier lifestyle. They believed that with the right marketing and support, this activity could resonate with people and create a new market for running shoes.

Bill Bowerman, a track and field coach at the University of Oregon, was passionate about fitness and had a deep understanding of the benefits of running. He co-authored a book titled "Jogging" in 1966, which served as a seminal piece of literature that brought attention to this emerging form of exercise. The book provided valuable insights into the benefits of jogging, making it more accessible to the general public and dispelling misconceptions about its effects.

Around the same time, Phil Knight, an entrepreneur and former track athlete, co-founded Blue Ribbon Sports, later renamed Nike. Knight shared Bowerman's belief in the power of jogging as a way to improve overall well-being. He recognized that by educating customers about the importance of fitness and jogging, they could create a new market for running shoes that catered to the specific needs of joggers.

Phil Knight and Bowerman embarked on a mission to actively promote the benefits of jogging through various marketing campaigns and endorsements. They emphasized how jogging could lead to better health, increased fitness, and a more balanced lifestyle. As they continued to educate the public about the advantages of jogging, they also developed innovative running shoes designed to enhance the jogging experience.

Their combined efforts paid off, and the popularity of jogging began to soar. More and more people started to embrace this form of exercise as they became aware of its positive impact on their well-being. With Nike's innovative running shoes and the continuous promotion of jogging's benefits, the once niche activity evolved into a widespread fitness trend.

Through the unwavering dedication of Bowerman, Knight, and others, jogging became a symbol of a healthier lifestyle. Their visionary approach and relentless education efforts transformed jogging from an unfamiliar concept to a mainstream activity embraced by millions worldwide.

This inspiring example of how jogging became a global fitness trend highlights one of the limitations of the Jobs to be Done (JTBD) framework.

When Bowerman and Knight embarked on their journey to promote jogging, they were not responding to existing customer needs or demands. Instead, they envisioned a future where jogging could revolutionize people's approach to health and wellness.

Had they solely relied on JTBD, their efforts might have been limited to addressing current customer preferences and immediate needs. The framework is excellent for understanding customers' present requirements and optimizing products accordingly. However, it may not have been sufficient to predict the surge in demand for jogging or create a new market around this activity.

"Nike: Turning couch potatoes into running tomatoes, one pair of shoes at a time!" 😄

03 Psychological Factors

The Jobs to be Done (JTBD) framework may not fully capture the complex psychological factors that drive customer behaviour. While JTBD can be a valuable tool for understanding customers' needs and motivations, it may not consider the role of subconscious cues and emotional associations that drive customer behaviour.

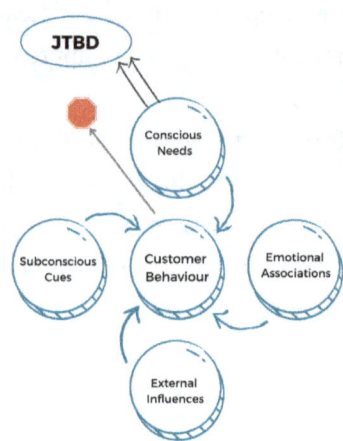

Conscious Needs

These are the explicit and rational needs that customers are aware of and actively seek to fulfill. The JTBD framework can effectively capture these conscious needs, as it focuses on understanding the specific jobs customers want to accomplish.

Subconscious Cues

These are subtle signals or triggers that impact customer behavior on a subconscious level. They may include visual cues, branding, and other sensory elements that influence decision-making.

Emotional Associations

Emotions play a significant role in customer behavior. Positive emotions can lead to loyalty and repeat purchases, while negative emotions can deter customers from a brand or product.

External Influences

Customers are influenced by external factors such as social trends, peer opinions, environmental stimulus, and cultural norms.

JTBD cannot fully capture critical aspects of Subconscious Cues, Emotional Associations, and External Influences

Fast Food Chain—The fast food industry constantly strives to meet its customers' changing needs and preferences. In one such instance, a fast food chain conducted extensive research to understand what customers wanted to accomplish when they came to their restaurant. They used various research techniques, including observational research and open-ended interviews and identified that customers were becoming more health-conscious and seeking healthier menu options. In response, the fast food chain developed a low-carb and low-fat sandwich and tested it with a focus group. The results were overwhelmingly positive, and the fast food chain invested heavily in promoting the product, expecting a massive boost in sales.

However, despite the initial positive response, sandwich sales started declining. The fast food chain was perplexed about why the product was not selling as expected. They discovered that the Jobs to be Done framework they used in their research had limitations. While customers expressed a desire to eat healthy food, they were ultimately influenced by subconscious cues and emotional associations when purchasing.

They discovered that the customers' subconscious mind was influencing their decision-making process. When people visited the fast food chain for lunch, visual images of advertisements and banners inside the restaurant and the smell of the food acted as cues. Customers tended to order something they had already ordered before, even if their rational minds wanted to try a healthier option. Their subconscious mind often made the decision, and sensory cues were connected to emotional memories, bringing back pleasant experiences associated with their preferred orders.

"Trying to sell a healthy sandwich at a fast food joint is like asking a French fry to go for a jog - it's just not their thing!"

A New Cola Brand—One big brand decided to venture into the cola market, aiming to launch a new cola beverage to compete against the market leader. Before proceeding, they conducted thorough user research to understand the "jobs" that consumers wanted to be done when consuming cola. The research revealed key motivations, including quenching thirst, desiring a beverage with less sugar and seeking a refreshing and enjoyable taste experience.

Armed with this valuable insight, the brand developed a new cola product that addressed these specific needs. They conducted blind taste tests with focus groups, and to their delight, the new cola beverage consistently outperformed the market leader's product. The feedback was overwhelmingly positive, reinforcing the belief that they had a superior product on their hands.

With confidence in their new product, the brand launched it on a mass scale in multiple regions simultaneously. They initiated an extensive marketing campaign to create a mass frenzy around the launch, offering attractive discounts and carrying out various promotional activities.

Initially, the response to the new cola was promising, and it garnered attention from consumers. However, to the brand's dismay, after a few days, the sales started declining rapidly. Even after a minor dip, the market leader's cola sales bounced back to normal levels.

Perplexed by the sudden decline in their product's performance, the brand's team sought to understand the underlying reasons behind this phenomenon.

It became evident that the Jobs to be Done (JTBD) framework they relied upon had limitations in explaining the consumers' decision-making process accurately.

The consumers' decision-making process is not entirely rational, as we might like to believe. The intuitive mind, or the subconscious mind, plays a significant role in influencing our choices, often more than the rational mind. When consumers encounter a brand, their subconscious mind immediately activates learned cultural associations, memories, and habits associated with that brand.

In the case of cola beverages, the market leader's brand, like Coke or Pepsi, carries deep-rooted associations formed over a long period of time. It is instantly recognizable and has a strong emotional appeal due to its rich history of advertising and cultural significance. The consumers' rational minds may not always be able to explain exactly why they prefer a particular product, as many of their feelings and preferences are connected to the subconscious mind.

In focus group settings, the rational mind tends to be more active due to the new environment, the feeling of being observed, the presence of unknown participants, and the possibility of embarrassment. Consequently, consumers may rationalize their thoughts and provide logical reasoning during such sessions. However, their true feelings and emotional connections lie in the subconscious mind, which heavily influences their actual purchasing behaviour.

As a result, the positive feedback received in the focus groups may not be an accurate measure of the new product's success in the real world. The brand's superior taste and lower sugar content, while significant attributes, were not enough to overcome the strong emotional associations consumers had with the market leader's brand.

This example underscores the limitation of the JTBD framework in fully capturing the role of subconscious cues and emotional associations in consumer decision-making. By understanding and leveraging these emotional connections, brands can create more effective strategies to meet customer expectations and drive successful product launches. In this case, the brand's new cola faced challenges in breaking the deeply ingrained consumer preferences and emotional attachments associated with the market leader's brand, resulting in declining sales despite the initial positive feedback.

04 Sell Experiences

In today's highly competitive market, it's not enough to meet the customer's functional needs; brands need to create an emotional connection and memorable moments that resonate with customers on a deeper level. This is where selling experiences come in.

Here are some reasons why selling experiences is critical:

1. **Emotional Engagement**: Experiences evoke emotions, and emotions play a significant role in shaping customers' perceptions and decisions. When customers have positive emotional experiences with a brand, they are more likely to form a strong attachment and become loyal advocates.
2. **Brand Loyalty**: Building emotional connections with customers through experiences fosters brand loyalty. Loyal customers are more likely to make repeat purchases, refer the brand to others, and withstand competitive offers.
3. **Differentiation**: In markets where products are commoditized, experiences provide a way for brands to differentiate themselves from the competition. Customers are willing to pay more for a product or service that delivers an exceptional experience.
4. **Customer Satisfaction**: Satisfied customers are more likely to become loyal customers and generate positive word-of-mouth. An excellent experience leaves a lasting impression, increasing the likelihood of repeat business.
5. **Brand Reputation**: Positive experiences contribute to a strong brand reputation. Word-of-mouth and online reviews from delighted customers enhance a brand's credibility and attract new customers.

6. **Word-of-Mouth Marketing**: Customers who have had exceptional experiences are more likely to share their experiences with friends, family, and on social media. Word-of-mouth marketing is powerful, as people trust recommendations from their peers.

7. **Customer Retention**: Selling experiences increase customer retention rates. When customers feel emotionally connected to a brand, they are less likely to switch to a competitor.

8. **Customer Advocacy**: Loyal customers who have had positive experiences often become brand advocates, promoting the brand voluntarily. They defend the brand during crises and actively participate in brand-related discussions.

9. **Upselling and Cross-Selling**: Satisfied customers are more receptive to upselling and cross-selling efforts. They trust the brand's recommendations and are open to trying new products or services.

10. **Enhanced Customer Lifetime Value**: Customers who have positive experiences are more valuable to a business over their lifetime. They spend more, refer more, and require less marketing spend to retain.

11. **Emotional Resilience**: Customers who have a strong emotional connection with a brand are more likely to remain loyal during challenging times, such as economic downturns or product issues.

12. **Personalization**: Experiences allow for more personalized interactions with customers. By understanding their needs, preferences, and emotions, brands can tailor their offerings to match individual customer requirements.

How Brands Sell Experiences?

Case Study—Airbnb

Airbnb stands as a prime example of a company that goes beyond meeting functional needs to sell transformative experiences. It all began with the founders, Chesky and Gebbia, facing financial constraints and identifying a unique opportunity during a design conference in their city. Understanding the struggles of fellow designers seeking affordable accommodation, they decided to rent out a part of their home to conference attendees. This marked the inception of Airbnb, driven by a vision to offer personalized and delightful experiences to travellers.

Taking a customer-centric approach, Chesky and Gebbia sought to understand their guests' objectives and trip goals. They carefully curated the guest experience, starting with a thoughtful welcome package containing essentials like a BART pass, city maps, and even spare change to support the homeless. Breakfasts of untoasted Pop-Tarts and Orange juice were served, and they personally guided guests to local hotspots, including their favourite Taco place, Ferry Building, and Stanford's design school. These small gestures created a memorable and authentic experience that hotel stays couldn't replicate, forging genuine connections between guests and hosts.

Airbnb broadly delivers two types of experiences: Human Experience and Cultural Experience. The Human Experience centres around the intimate interactions between guests and hosts, fostering a sense of companionship and alleviating the feeling of solitude that travellers often experience. Guests become immersed in the local culture, making it akin to Chesky and Gebbia's friendship with their initial guests.

The Cultural Experience offered by Airbnb allows travellers to delve into new places as locals do, providing a personalized and authentic journey. This essence was captured brilliantly in Airbnb's marketing campaign, "Don't Go There. Live There." The campaign emphasized a deeper connection to the community and a desire to genuinely experience the places they visit.

Both guests and hosts gain cultural experiences through Airbnb's platform. Hosts have the opportunity to connect with people from diverse backgrounds and learn about their guests' lives and travel experiences. This mutual exchange strengthens the community and fosters lasting friendships.

Key Factors Enabling Airbnb's Exceptional Customer Experiences

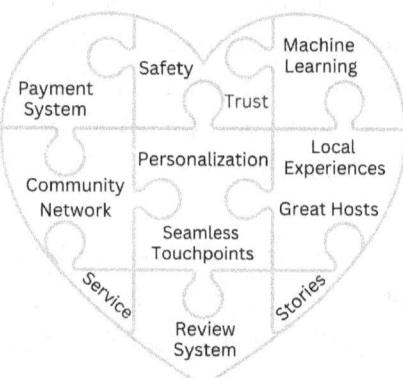

Here is a list of some of the experiences Airbnb Offers:

1. **Unique and Personalized Accommodations:** One of the key ways Airbnb

sells experiences is by offering unique and personalized accommo-dations. Unlike traditional hotels, where rooms can feel generic and impersonal, Airbnb listings are often distinct and reflect the personality and style of the hosts. Customers can choose from a variety of options, such as cosy cottages, stylish apartments, or charming villas, making their stay more memorable and tailored to their preferences.

2. **Emphasis on Local Experiences:** Airbnb goes beyond providing a place to stay; it encourages travellers to immerse themselves in local culture and experiences. Through its "Experiences" feature, Airbnb offers a range of activities and tours hosted by locals. This allows travellers to engage with the local community, learn about their traditions, and explore unique aspects of the destination they wouldn't typically find in guidebooks.

3. **User-Generated Content:** Airbnb leverages user-generated content to showcase real experiences shared by previous guests. Customer reviews, ratings, and photos provide social proof and build trust among potential guests, making them more likely to choose an accommodation based on positive experiences shared by others.

4. **Storytelling and Emotional Appeal:** Airbnb's marketing campaigns focus on storytelling and evoke emotions. Their advertisements often depict heartwarming stories of hosts and guests, forming connections and creating lasting memories. By using storytelling, Airbnb taps into the emotional aspect of travel, making customers feel that they are not just booking a place to stay but embarking on an adventure and making meaningful connections.

5. **Seamless Booking Process:** Airbnb provides a user-friendly and seam-less booking process, making it easy for customers to find and reserve accommodations. The platform's intuitive design and transparent pricing contribute to a positive user experience, enhancing the overall perception of the brand.

6. **Community Building:** Airbnb has successfully built a community of hosts and guests worldwide. Hosts actively engage with guests, providing tips and recommendations, which creates a sense of belonging

and a shared community experience. This community-driven approach fosters a sense of loyalty and encourages repeat bookings.

7. **Social Impact:** Airbnb's "Open Homes" initiative allows hosts to offer their homes for free to people in need during times of crisis. This commitment to social impact resonates with customers who appreciate the brand's efforts to make a positive difference in the world.

8. **Safety Factor:** Safety is a critical factor in selling experiences, especially in the travel and hospitality industry. Airbnb recognized early on that ensuring the safety and security of both hosts and guests was paramount to building trust and credibility. They implemented various safety measures, including a robust verification process for hosts and guests, secure payment systems, and a review system that allows users to provide feedback on their experiences. By prioritizing safety, Airbnb creates a sense of comfort and reassurance for customers, making them more willing to book accommodations and engage in experiences on the platform.

9. **Trust:** Trust is the foundation of any successful experience-based business. Airbnb's focus on building trust between hosts and guests is a key driver in selling experiences. Through the review system and user-generated content, Airbnb establishes transparency and accountability. Guests can read reviews from previous guests, gaining insights into the quality of the accommodations and the hospitality of the hosts. This social proof builds trust, as potential guests can make informed decisions based on the experiences of others.

10. **Network Effect:** The network effect is a powerful mechanism that contributes to the success of selling experiences on Airbnb. As more hosts join the platform, the variety and availability of accommodations increase, attracting a larger pool of potential guests. Simultaneously, more guests create demand for accommodations, incentivizing more hosts to list their spaces. This virtuous cycle strengthens the platform's value proposition, making it the go-to choice for travellers seeking unique and personalized experiences.

11. **Payment System:** Airbnb's secure and convenient payment system

was a game-changer compared to traditional methods of booking accommodations. By providing a seamless and reliable payment process, Airbnb eliminated friction in the booking journey, making it easier and more efficient for customers to make reservations. The ease of payment adds to the overall positive experience, encouraging customers to return to the platform for future bookings.

12. **Delivering Experiences at Every Touchpoint:** From the moment a potential guest lands on the Airbnb website or app, the brand focuses on delivering a seamless and delightful experience at every touchpoint. The user-friendly interface, intuitive search options, and personalized recommendations ensure that customers can easily find accommodations that match their preferences. Airbnb also emphasizes local experiences through its "Experiences" feature, offering curated activities hosted by locals. This focus on delivering experiences at every touchpoint creates a holistic and immersive journey for customers, making them feel connected to the destination and the culture.

13. **Machine Learning:** Machine learning is a critical component of Airbnb's ability to deliver exceptional customer experiences. It enables personalized recommendations, dynamic pricing, and improved search results, ensuring guests find the perfect accommodations quickly. Machine learning also enhances safety by detecting and preventing fraud, while AI-powered chatbots provide instant customer support. The analysis of guest reviews and image recognition further contributes to optimizing listings and providing valuable insights. By predicting travel demand and facilitating language translation, machine learning ensures a seamless and globally connected experience for customers on the platform.

By prioritizing experiences and connections over mere transactions, Airbnb has redefined the travel industry. It has shown that successful businesses not only fulfill functional needs but also create emotional bonds with customers, turning them into loyal brand advocates. Through personalization, community building, storytelling, and a focus on local experiences, Airbnb has set the benchmark for selling experiences rather than just products.

Airbnb and JTBD Framework Limitations in Selling Experiences

Airbnb's exceptional focus on selling experiences instead of merely meeting functional needs highlights the limitations of the Jobs to be Done (JTBD) framework in addressing the complexities of delivering such experiences.

Inadequate Emphasis on Emotional and Experiential Aspects: While JTBD proves valuable in understanding customers' functional needs and motivations, it falls short in capturing the emotional and experiential aspects that drive customer behaviour in the travel and hospitality industry. Experiences are highly subjective and vary from person to person, making it challenging for JTBD to fully capture the diverse emotional drivers influencing customer decisions. Moreover, the framework's focus on functional needs might overlook the profound desire for adventure, exploration, and cultural immersion that guests seek in their travel experiences. Understanding these emotional aspects is crucial as they play a significant role in shaping customer decisions and fostering loyalty.

Cultural Experience: One of Airbnb's core offerings is the cultural experience, where customers yearn to immerse themselves in diverse cultures during their stays. In fact, before Airbnb, only a few people were exposed to the idea of staying in local cultures while travelling. However, Airbnb disrupted the traditional hospitality industry by creating a need and desire for such experiences, exposing several people to the concept of living like a local. By fostering authentic interactions with local communities, Airbnb satisfies the profound hidden desire of guests to connect with the essence of their travel destinations.

Overlooking the Significance of Hosts in Delivering Experiences: Airbnb's success is not only attributed to its cultural experiences but also to the pivotal role played by its hosts in delivering personalized and unique guest experiences. However, the Jobs to be Done (JTBD) framework might not fully grasp the significance of hosts as a separate customer segment, overlooking their contribution to fostering emotional connections and creating memorable stays for guests.

The presence of hosts within the Airbnb ecosystem creates a sense of belonging and community for guests, elevating their experience beyond a mere transaction. Hosts offer a warm and personal touch, generously sharing their local knowledge, culture, and traditions, enriching the guest's stay. They create a welcoming environment that makes guests feel at home, even in a foreign place.

Hosts are more than just property owners; they act as cultural ambassadors, passionately sharing their love for their city or region with travelers. Through these authentic human connections, guests can delve deeper into their travel destination, gaining a profound appreciation for the local culture and way of life. This level of engagement sets Airbnb apart from traditional accommodation options and is not fully captured by the JTBD framework, which might not recognize the emotional significance of such human interactions.

The platform's success lies in its ability to foster genuine and meaningful interactions between hosts and guests, ensuring that guests feel cared for, understood, and valued. This human touch enhances the overall travel experience, making it memorable and special.

Limitations of JTBD in Delivering Seamless Experience Across All Touch-points: One of Airbnb's key success factors is its ability to consistently deliver a seamless experience for customers across all touchpoints. However, when applying the Jobs-to-be-Done (JTBD) framework, there are several limitations to ensuring this level of seamlessness throughout the customer journey. These limitations include:

1. Lack of granularity: The JTBD framework focuses on understanding the high-level job that customers want to accomplish. While this provides valuable insights into the customer's main goal, it might not capture the finer details and specific interactions required for a seamless experience at each touchpoint.

2. Incomplete customer journey view: JTBD might not encompass the

entire customer journey, including all touchpoints and interactions. This can lead to gaps in understanding customer needs and expectations at crucial stages, hindering the ability to create a coherent and seamless experience.

3. Limited real-time adaptability: Personalized and seamless experiences often require real-time adaptability based on the customer's current context and behaviour. The retrospective nature of the JTBD framework may not facilitate real-time adjustments at various touchpoints.

4. Ignoring channel-specific nuances: Different touchpoints often come with unique characteristics and requirements. The JTBD framework might not adequately consider these channel-specific nuances, making it challenging to deliver consistent experiences across various touchpoints.

5. Overlooking emotional and experiential factors: Seamlessness is not only about meeting functional needs but also about addressing emotional and experiential aspects. JTBD may not fully capture the emotional triggers and experiential elements that play a significant role in shaping a seamless customer experience.

6. Integrating data and systems: To deliver a seamless experience, data from various touchpoints and systems must be integrated and analyzed. JTBD alone might not provide guidance on how to effectively collect and combine data to achieve seamless personalization.

7. Addressing cross-channel challenges: Customers often interact with a brand through multiple channels, and delivering a seamless experience requires a unified approach across these channels. JTBD might not inherently address the complexities of delivering a consistent experience in a cross-channel environment.

8. Limited segmentation insights: Personalization often involves tailoring experiences to specific customer segments. While JTBD helps identify core needs, it might not provide detailed insights into the preferences and behaviours of different customer segments, hindering effective personalization efforts.

In summary, while JTBD is a valuable framework for understanding functional needs, it may not have fully captured the intricate emotional, experiential, and community-driven aspects that underpin Airbnb's success in selling experiences.

05 Difficulty in Identifying the Right Job

Identifying the right job that customers are trying to accomplish is a significant challenge businesses often face when developing products or services.

"Sometimes, using JTBD to identify the right job feels like searching for a unicorn in a job market full of donkeys. It's mythical!"

Pinpointing the precise job using JBTD can be complex for several reasons:

a) Diverse Customer Needs

Customers have diverse needs, preferences, and motivations, which can vary greatly even within a specific target market. Identifying a single "job" that satisfies all customers can be challenging, as different individuals may have distinct use cases for the same product or service.

Let's consider a smartphone as the product in question. The "job" that customers want to accomplish with a smartphone can vary significantly based on their diverse needs, preferences, and motivations:

Example: Smartphone Usage for Different Customers

1. Business Professional: A business professional might use a smartphone primarily for productivity-related tasks, such as checking emails,

scheduling appointments, and managing documents. Their main job is to stay organized and connected while on the go.

2. Tech Enthusiast: A tech-savvy individual may view a smartphone as a platform for exploring the latest apps, games, and cutting-edge features. Their main job is to stay up-to-date with technology trends and enjoy the latest innovations.

3. Fitness Enthusiast: For a fitness enthusiast, a smartphone can be a fitness tracker and workout companion. Their main job is to monitor their health, track workouts, and access fitness-related apps.

4. Social Media Influencer: A social media influencer may see a smartphone as a tool for content creation, editing photos and videos, and engaging with their audience on various social platforms. Their main job is to create and share captivating content.

5. Senior Citizen: An elderly user might use a smartphone primarily for communication with family and friends, making video calls, and accessing basic features like a calculator or reminders. Their main job is to stay connected with loved ones and perform essential tasks conveniently.

6. Student: A student's main job with a smartphone might involve research, studying, note-taking, and accessing educational resources. Their main job is to support their academic pursuits.

As we can see from these examples, different customers have distinct use cases and priorities when using a smartphone. Identifying a single job that encompasses all these diverse needs and motivations can be challenging for businesses.

b) Evolving Customer Expectations

Customer needs and expectations evolve over time due to changing circumstances, technological advancements, or external factors. What might have been the primary job a few years ago might not hold the same relevance today.

The Case of Personal Transportation: A few years ago, when the JTBD framework was applied to personal transportation, it might have led to the identification of the primary job as "getting from point A to point B efficiently." In response to this job, the market developed solutions like traditional taxis and car ownership.

However, as time progressed, so did customer needs and expectations. Technological advancements gave birth to ridesharing services and on-demand transportation apps, which not only fulfilled the primary job but also introduced additional jobs such as "safety," "convenience," and "cost-effectiveness." These new expectations were largely driven by the changing landscape of personal transportation, including concerns about the environment, the desire for real-time information, and the need for seamless, cashless transactions.

In this evolving scenario, the JTBD framework's initial definition of the primary job falls short, as it fails to account for the nuanced needs of the modern customer. While the traditional approach to personal transportation still serves a purpose, it no longer fully addresses the complex landscape of customer expectations.

The JTBD framework, rooted in a static understanding of customer needs, tends to categorize the primary job as a fixed concept. It does not easily adapt to the evolving nature of customer expectations and the introduction of new variables that affect their choices.

Customers today are not merely looking for transportation; they seek experiences that align with their values, preferences, and changing circumstances. JTBD, which initially defined the job in a different context, does not adequately account for these shifts. This can lead businesses to overlook critical opportunities, as they continue to target the original, outdated job, while ignoring the more intricate and multifaceted set of jobs that customers now need to be done.

Music Streaming: When music streaming first emerged, the primary job customers wanted to be done was simple: access music on demand. The initial platforms like Pandora and early versions of Spotify succeeded in delivering this job effectively. They allowed users to stream an extensive library of music at their convenience, thus satisfying their immediate needs.

However, as time went by, customer expectations evolved, introducing a multitude of new jobs within the music streaming ecosystem. These jobs included:

1. **Discovering New Music:** Customers began to seek platforms that could help them discover new artists and songs tailored to their individual tastes.
2. **Personalization:** Users expected platforms to adapt to their listening habits, offering playlists and recommendations that felt truly personalized.
3. **Offline Listening:** With an increase in mobility, the ability to download and listen to music offline became a crucial job for many users.
4. **High-Quality Audio:** As technology improved, so did the desire for higher audio quality, resulting in the need for lossless and high-definition streaming.
5. **Social Integration:** Social sharing and interaction around music became a new job, as users wanted to connect with friends and share their musical preferences.

The JTBD framework, when applied to music streaming, initially captured the primary job as "accessing music on demand." However, it did not anticipate the rapid emergence of these new jobs, nor did it account for the dynamic nature of evolving customer needs. JTBD's limitation lies in its static definition of the primary job, which assumes a single, unchanging job to be done.

As a result, JTBD-led platforms that focus solely on the primary job may neglect these evolving needs, leaving customers dissatisfied and seeking alternatives. This limitation is particularly evident in the case of businesses that fail to provide personalized recommendations, high-quality audio, or offline listening options.

c) Unarticulated Needs

Customers may not always be able to articulate their needs accurately or may not even be aware of certain needs until presented with a solution. Traditional market research and customer feedback might not fully capture these unarticulated needs, leading to a potential misalignment in product development.

The Rise of Wearable Fitness: The fitness industry is a prime example of how the 'Jobs To Be Done' (JTBD) framework can overlook unarticulated customer needs. While customers may have some explicit needs related to fitness, they may not always be able to express more nuanced or evolving needs until they encounter a solution. Traditional market research and customer feedback may not capture these unarticulated needs, leading to potential shortcomings in product development.

Several years ago, fitness tracking devices and wearable technology started gaining popularity. The primary job customers explicitly wanted to be done was tracking their physical activity and monitoring their health. This need was relatively straightforward, and early fitness trackers like pedometers aimed to fulfill it.

However, as the technology evolved, new, unarticulated customer needs emerged:

1. **Heart Rate Monitoring:** Customers initially focused on step counts but later revealed unarticulated needs for heart rate monitoring as they became more health-conscious.
2. **Sleep Tracking:** Tracking sleep patterns was an unarticulated need that became evident when customers realized the impact of sleep on their overall health and fitness goals.
3. **Nutritional Insights:** While initially not a part of the primary job, customers began to express unarticulated needs for nutritional insights and diet tracking as they recognized the role of nutrition in achieving their fitness goals.

4. **Stress Management:** The impact of stress on overall health was an unarticulated need that only emerged when wearable devices began offering stress tracking features.

The JTBD framework, relying on traditional market research and customer feedback, may have primarily identified the primary job as tracking physical activity and monitoring health. As a result, it might have overlooked these unarticulated needs because customers were not fully aware of them until presented with the technology that could fulfill them.

Traditional research methods often operate based on current customer preferences and expectations and can miss emerging needs. The JTBD framework's static definition of the primary job can hinder its ability to anticipate unarticulated needs related to evolving technology and changing customer behaviors.

Addressing these unarticulated needs can lead to higher customer satisfaction, improved product performance, and increased market adoption. It also demonstrates the importance of continuously monitoring customer experiences to stay ahead of evolving preferences and expectations. Companies that actively seek out and address unarticulated needs are more likely to create successful products that resonate with their customers on a deeper level.

The Smartphone Revolution: In the early 2000s, the mobile phone industry was dominated by feature phones, and customer needs appeared well-defined: making calls, sending texts, and perhaps some basic web browsing. The Jobs To Be Done at that time were centered around communication and limited internet access.

Enter the smartphone, a revolutionary product that disrupted the status quo by introducing a myriad of features and capabilities that customers hadn't explicitly articulated as needs:

1. **App Ecosystem:** The introduction of app stores and a vast ecosystem of mobile applications presented a new world of unarticulated needs. Users couldn't have foreseen their desire for everything from ride-sharing

apps to calorie counters until these solutions became available.

2. **Touchscreen Technology:** Before smartphones, customers had no clear way of articulating their desire for touchscreen devices, which brought forth a more intuitive and user-friendly interface.

3. **Multimedia Capabilities:** Unarticulated needs related to photo and video sharing, music streaming, and on-the-go entertainment came to the forefront with the advent of smartphones.

4. **Location-Based Services:** The concept of using your device for real-time navigation, which was previously unarticulated, became a standard feature in smartphones.

5. **Personal Assistants:** Virtual personal assistants like Siri and Google Assistant anticipated unarticulated needs for voice-activated commands and integrated search functionalities.

The JTBD framework, when relying on traditional market research and customer feedback, might have identified the need for communication and basic internet access but would have missed these unarticulated, emerging needs. Customers couldn't have explicitly requested features like app stores or personal assistants because they weren't even aware such possibilities existed.

d) Conflicting Requirements

In some cases, customers might have conflicting requirements when using a product. For example, they may desire a feature that enhances convenience but also seek one that provides maximum security, creating a challenge in finding a balanced solution.

Consider the example of a washing machine, a household appliance central to daily life. Customers have historically articulated their primary job for washing machines as "efficiently cleaning clothes while saving time."

However, the modern home appliance landscape has introduced new requirements, including environmentally friendly operation and safety:

1. **Convenience Requirement:** Customers prioritize washing machines that offer quick cycles, enabling them to clean their clothes swiftly and efficiently. They desire features like express wash settings and large load capacities to save time and effort.

2. **Environmental Requirement:** Simultaneously, there's an emerging unarticulated need for environmentally conscious appliances that minimize water and energy consumption. Customers are increasingly concerned about the ecological impact of their household choices.

3. **Safety Requirement:** A further unarticulated need emerges for safety features that prevent accidents and mishaps, particularly for families with children. Customers seek appliances with secure locks, childproof settings, and hazard prevention mechanisms.

The JTBD framework, when relying on traditional market research and customer feedback, may have captured the primary job related to efficient clothes cleaning. However, it could face difficulties in addressing conflicting requirements, particularly the challenge of balancing convenience, environmental impact, and safety in a single product.

e) Overlapping Jobs

Customers may use a product or service to accomplish multiple jobs simultaneously. Understanding the hierarchy of these jobs and their interdependencies is crucial for providing a comprehensive solution.

The smart home industry provides an illuminating example of how the 'Jobs To Be Done' (JTBD) framework may face challenges when customers use a product to accomplish multiple jobs simultaneously. Recognizing the hierarchy of these jobs and their interdependencies is crucial for offering a comprehensive solution.

Consider a smart thermostat, designed to provide energy efficiency, comfort, and convenience. Customers have several jobs they want to be done simultaneously:

1. **Energy Efficiency:** Customers desire a smart thermostat to optimize their home's heating and cooling systems, reducing energy consumption, and consequently, utility bills.
2. **Comfort:** At the same time, they want their smart thermostat to maintain a comfortable temperature, ensuring they enjoy a cozy living environment.
3. **Convenience:** Customers also expect their smart thermostat to be remotely controllable via smartphone apps, allowing them to adjust settings when they're away from home, providing convenience.

The JTBD framework, rooted in the definition of a primary job, may encounter challenges when it comes to overlapping jobs with interdependencies. It might be adept at addressing one job, but not necessarily the others. For instance:

· While the smart thermostat could excel in optimizing energy efficiency by using data and machine learning, it may not prioritize comfort or convenience.
· A focus on comfort might lead to temperature settings that are not energy-efficient.
· Prioritizing convenience could lead to remote control features but not necessarily optimized energy use or the coziest temperatures.

Customers often expect smart thermostats to tackle all these jobs simultaneously, understanding that they are interconnected. For instance, optimizing energy efficiency may involve adjusting the temperature slightly to save energy, which could impact comfort. Similarly, the convenience of remote control should not compromise energy efficiency.

Understanding the hierarchy of these overlapping jobs and their interdependencies is crucial for providing a comprehensive solution that balances all these requirements. In many cases, businesses may struggle to harmonize these jobs, resulting in a product that satisfies one aspect while neglecting others.

f) Difficulty in Prioritizing Customer Needs

Another limitation of the JTBD framework is the difficulty in prioritizing customer needs. While the framework can help identify a range of customer needs and jobs to be done, it may not provide clear guidance on which needs are the most important or urgent to address. This is because different customers may have different needs and priorities, and it can be challenging for companies to determine which needs are the most important or urgent to address.

For example, a company that develops healthcare products may use the JTBD framework to identify a range of customer needs for managing chronic conditions. However, they may struggle to prioritize which needs to address first, given that some needs may be more urgent or have a greater impact on customer quality of life or have a greater impact on customer satisfaction or loyalty.

In addition, different customers may have different needs and priorities at certain times, making it challenging to develop a one-size-fits-all solution. This can make it difficult for companies to allocate resources effectively and develop products that meet the most pressing customer needs.

g) Overemphasis on Individual Needs

Another limitation of the JTBD framework is the potential overemphasis on individual needs, which may not always align with broader societal or environmental concerns. While the JTBD framework can be useful for understanding customer needs and preferences, it may not guide how to balance these needs with broader social or environmental considerations.

For example, a company may use the JTBD framework to identify a customer need for a convenient and easy-to-use single-use product. However, the production and disposal of this product may have negative environmental impacts, which may not be immediately apparent to the customer.

In addition, focusing too narrowly on individual needs may not address broader societal concerns such as equity, access, or sustainability. For example, a healthcare company that focuses solely on meeting the needs of wealthy patients may not address the healthcare needs of underserved communities.

06 Limited Scope

JTBD may not always provide a broader view of the customer's overall lifestyle, preferences, and attitudes. This can limit the insights gained from JTBD and result in incomplete or inaccurate conclusions about customer needs and motivations.

"Imagine understanding someone's entire life story based on a single selfie. That's JTBD - it captures a moment, but life is a whole movie."

Let's explore this limitation through a detailed example.

Consider the scenario of someone shopping for a coffee machine. They articulate their primary job to be done as "making a morning coffee quickly and conveniently." This simple, explicit need might lead to the purchase of a basic coffee maker that serves this specific purpose efficiently. However, the Jobs to be Done (JTBD) framework, when relying on traditional market research and customer feedback, can sometimes fall short of uncovering the broader context that significantly influences the product's design, styling, and appeal.

Let's break down how the broader context, including lifestyle, preferences, attitudes, and emotional needs, plays a pivotal role in guiding product styling and enhancing the overall customer experience:

Lifestyle: When a customer states their primary job to be done as "making a morning coffee quickly and conveniently," it's only a glimpse into their daily routine. However, a more comprehensive understanding of their lifestyle reveals that coffee serves multiple roles. For instance, they might lead a busy life and need a coffee machine that delivers efficiency in the morning. But beyond that, on weekends or when hosting guests, their lifestyle might involve socializing or relaxing over cups of coffee. For these occasions, a coffee machine that caters to larger groups is more suitable. Therefore, the product design should consider the versatility to accommodate different aspects of the customer's lifestyle.

A person's lifestyle choices also play a significant role in guiding the styling of a product. For example, individuals with a minimalistic lifestyle often favour products with a clean and uncluttered design. Minimalistic design is characterized by simplicity, functionality, and an emphasis on essential elements.

Preferences: While the basic need is for a quick morning coffee, the customer's preferences regarding coffee styles come into play. Some coffee enthusiasts prefer espressos for that intense flavor kick, while others enjoy cappuccinos or lattes with frothy milk. The product design should cater to these preferences. For example, having the option for various coffee styles or including a milk frother can greatly enhance the appeal of the coffee machine.

Attitudes: Understanding a customer's attitudes and values is a pivotal aspect of product design, extending beyond their primary job to be done. Customers exhibit diverse attitudes, and recognizing and aligning with these values can significantly broaden a product's appeal. Here are a few examples of how attitudes guide product styling and marketing initiatives, making it relevant to a wider customer base:

Some customers prioritize sustainability and eco-friendliness. For them, an environmentally conscious coffee machine that's energy-efficient and eco-friendly may be a decisive factor in their purchase. The product design can incorporate sustainable materials, recyclable components, and energy-saving features, catering to these values. This approach resonates with customers who want their coffee experience to align with their environmental concerns.

Individuals with a strong inclination towards self-reliance may seek coffee machines that emphasize autonomy. Product styling in such cases highlights features like user-friendly controls, customizable brewing options, and easy maintenance. This approach makes users feel in control of their coffee-making process, empowering them to brew coffee exactly as they prefer. Marketing initiatives can emphasize the freedom and independence this product provides for making café-quality coffee at home.

For those enthusiastic about technology, product styling can embrace modern and sleek designs. High-tech features like app connectivity, touch-screen interfaces, and the use of polished, futuristic materials cater to this attitude. Marketing efforts can highlight the coffee machine's cutting-edge technology, focusing on the convenience and innovation that tech-savvy users can enjoy.

Customers valuing tradition may prefer a coffee machine with a classic, vintage appearance. The styling can incorporate elements that evoke a sense of nostalgia, such as retro colors or old-fashioned design accents. Marketing initiatives can tap into feelings of nostalgia, emphasizing how the coffee machine brings a touch of tradition to modern life. This approach resonates with customers who find comfort and familiarity in the aesthetics of the past.

Incorporating these varying attitudes into product design and marketing ensures that the product can cater to a broad and diverse customer base. It extends the product's appeal beyond its primary function, making it a reflection of the customer's values, and thereby enhancing its overall desirability.

Emotional Needs: Coffee is not just about caffeine; it's an integral part of daily rituals for many. It can symbolize comfort, relaxation, or motivation. Understanding these emotional needs and incorporating them into the product styling can be a game-changer. The textures, colors, and design elements of the coffee machine should evoke positive emotions and create an inviting experience. For example, a sleek, modern design may attract customers looking for a stylish addition to their kitchen, while a more rustic design can appeal to those seeking a cozy and familiar vibe.

The JTBD framework, when relying on traditional market research and customer feedback, may primarily capture the primary job in isolation, without delving into the broader context of lifestyle, preferences, attitudes, and emotional needs. As a result, the conclusions drawn might be too narrow to provide a comprehensive solution.

Customers expect their coffee machines to align with their overall lifestyle, preferences, and attitudes. A basic coffee maker, while excellent at quickly brewing a morning coffee, may fall short of meeting these broader expectations. In this case, JTBD's limited scope can lead to incomplete or inaccurate conclusions about what the customer truly needs.

07 Lack of Predictive Power

The Jobs to be Done (JTBD) framework is useful for understanding what customers try to accomplish when using a product. However, it is not a predictive tool and may not be able to predict future customer needs and behaviours accurately. This can limit its usefulness in creating long-term product strategies.

For example, a business may use JTBD to understand why customers hire their product to cook dinner. They may learn that customers hire their product to save time and effort in meal preparation. However, this understanding may not predict future changes in customer behaviour, such as a shift towards healthier eating or a growing interest in home-cooked meals. Without this predictive power, the business may miss opportunities to develop new products or improve its existing offerings to meet evolving customer needs.

Another example could be a company that develops a new smartphone based on customer feedback using JTBD. They may identify that customers are hiring their smartphones to accomplish the job of staying connected with friends and family. However, they may be unable to predict future changes in customer preferences or emerging technologies that could disrupt the smartphone market. This lack of predictive power can limit the company's ability to create a long-term product strategy that meets changing customer needs and preferences.

Kodak was once a dominant player in the photography industry but failed to anticipate the shift to digital photography. The company used JTBD to understand why customers were hiring their products — to capture and preserve memories. However, this understanding did not allow them to predict the rapid shift to digital photography, which fundamentally changed how people captured and stored images. Kodak's inability to predict this shift led to its decline and eventual bankruptcy.

08 Limited Use in Disruptive Innovation

JBTD framework may not be effective in identifying disruptive innovations that have the potential to transform an industry. This is because disruptive innovations often involve creating new markets or fundamentally changing how customers hire products, and JTBD may not fully capture these new needs and behaviours.

For example, consider the emergence of the smartphone. Before the smartphone, customers hired phones primarily for making calls and sending messages. The JTBD framework would have effectively identified these core needs and designed products that met them. However, the smartphone disrupted the market by creating new needs and behaviours, such as internet browsing, social media use, and mobile app usage. The JTBD framework did not capture these needs and behaviours, and businesses that relied solely on JTBD may have missed out on the potential for groundbreaking products in this new market.

Another example could be the emergence of ride-sharing services like Uber and Lyft. Before their introduction, customers hired taxis primarily for transportation from point A to point B. The JTBD framework would have effectively identified this core need and designed products that met it. However, ride-sharing services disrupted the market by creating new needs and behaviours, such as real-time ride tracking, in-app payments, and driver ratings. The JTBD framework did not fully capture these needs and behaviours, and businesses that relied solely on JTBD may have missed out on the potential for groundbreaking products in this new market.

09 Lack of Differentiation

JBTD framework may not be effective in helping companies differentiate their products from their competitors. This is because JTBD focuses on understanding the customer's core needs and does not necessarily provide insight into differentiating a product from others that may meet those same needs.

For example, consider a company that develops a new coffee maker using JTBD. They may learn that customers are hiring their coffee maker to make a quick, easy cup of coffee in the morning. However, this understanding may not provide insight into how to differentiate their coffee maker from others on the market that may also meet this need. Without differentiation, the company may struggle to stand out in the marketplace and attract customers.

Another example could be a company that develops a new fitness app using JTBD. They may learn that customers are hiring their app to track their workouts and progress. However, this understanding may not provide insight into how to differentiate their app from others on the market that may also meet this need. Without differentiation, the company may struggle to stand out in the marketplace and attract users.

10 Limited Applicability to B2B Markets

The "Jobs to be Done" framework may not fully address the complexities of B2B interactions and decision-making processes. Here are some key points to consider:

1. Multiple Stakeholders and Decision Makers: In B2B environments, purchase decisions are often made by multiple stakeholders, each with distinct roles and objectives. These stakeholders may include executives, managers, end-users, procurement teams, and technical experts.

The "Jobs to be Done" framework primarily focuses on understanding the needs and motivations of a single customer, which might not adequately capture the diverse and sometimes conflicting interests of various stakeholders involved in B2B purchases.

2. Longer Sales Cycles: B2B sales cycles are typically more extended and involve various stages, from identifying needs and solutions to negotiating contracts and ensuring long-term support.

The "Jobs to be Done" framework tends to emphasize identifying immediate customer needs and solving for them. However, B2B deals often involve long-term relationships and the need to address evolving needs over time, which goes beyond the framework's primary scope.

3. Solution Customization: B2B products and services are often highly customized to meet the specific requirements of clients. These customizations can extend beyond fulfilling immediate needs to integrating with existing systems, scaling to accommodate growth, and adhering to industry regulations.

The "Jobs to be Done" framework may not adequately address the complexity of customization and long-term adaptability required in B2B solutions.

4. Integration and Compatibility: B2B solutions need to seamlessly integrate with existing technologies and systems. Compatibility and ease of integration can be significant factors in the decision-making process.

The "Jobs to be Done" framework may not provide sufficient insights into integration requirements and compatibility issues, which are paramount in B2B settings.

5. Data-Driven Decision-Making: B2B decisions are often driven by data, ROI analysis, and in-depth feasibility studies. Companies prioritize solutions that offer quantifiable benefits and align with their strategic goals.

The "Jobs to be Done" framework, while valuable in uncovering qualitative customer needs, may lack the tools to address the rigorous data analysis and business case development typical in B2B environments.

6. Relationship-Centric Nature: B2B relationships extend beyond immediate transactions. Trust, ongoing support, and collaboration are essential components of B2B partnerships.

The "Jobs to be Done" framework primarily focuses on single transactions or jobs, potentially overlooking the need to build and maintain long-term relationships that are vital in B2B markets.

7. Industry Specificity: Different B2B industries have unique characteristics, regulations, and market dynamics. What constitutes a "job to be done" in one industry may differ significantly from another.

The framework may require extensive adaptation to cater to these industry-specific nuances, limiting its out-of-the-box applicability.

Addressing the diverse needs of multiple stakeholders, accommodating customization and integration, and aligning with data-driven decision-making are some of the challenges that need to be considered when utilizing the framework in B2B settings. Adaptations and complementary methodologies may be necessary to bridge the gap between the framework's core principles and the intricate landscape of B2B transactions.

11 Lack of Consideration for External Factors

The "Jobs to be Done" (JTBD) framework, which is primarily focused on understanding the fundamental jobs or tasks customers are trying to accomplish, can sometimes fall short in addressing the influence of external factors. These external factors, including economic, social, and technological forces, can significantly impact customer behavior and their choices. Here are some of the key points illustrating the limitation of the JTBD framework in this regard:

1. Economic Fluctuations: External economic conditions, such as recessions or economic booms, can have a profound effect on consumer behavior. During economic downturns, customers might prioritize cost savings and practicality, while in prosperous times, they may seek premium experiences and convenience.

The JTBD framework tends to focus on the internal motivations of customers, potentially overlooking the significant role that economic factors play in shaping their choices.

2. Cultural and Social Shifts: Changes in cultural and societal norms, values, and trends can lead to shifts in customer preferences and behaviors. For example, evolving attitudes towards sustainability, health, or social responsibility can influence purchase decisions.

The JTBD framework, which largely examines individual motivations, may not fully capture the broader cultural and social influences that drive customers' choices.

3. Technological Advancements: Rapid technological advancements often introduce new possibilities and disrupt established markets. Customers may be drawn to innovative solutions that were not previously available.

The JTBD framework primarily considers existing jobs and may not account for how technological changes can create entirely new jobs or alter the existing ones.

4. Regulatory Changes: Alterations in laws and regulations can impact the choices available to customers. For instance, new regulations may restrict certain products or promote alternatives.

The JTBD framework typically focuses on customer needs without delving into how external factors like regulatory changes can limit or expand those needs.

5. Competitive Landscape: The actions of competitors, including product launches, pricing strategies, and marketing campaigns, can significantly influence customer decisions.

While the JTBD framework helps understand customer needs, it may not fully address the competitive dynamics that shape the choices available to customers.

6. Global Events and Crises: Extraordinary events like pandemics, natural disasters, or geopolitical crises can lead to sudden shifts in customer behaviour. These events often prioritize safety, reliability, and preparedness.

The JTBD framework's focus on understanding customer motivations might not account for the unique demands and priorities that arise during such events.

7. Environmental Factors: Environmental factors such as climate change and resource scarcity can drive customers towards sustainable and eco-friendly choices. These considerations may become more critical in purchase decisions.

The JTBD framework's primary emphasis on individual needs may not fully recognize how global environmental concerns impact customer preferences.

To overcome this limitation, businesses must complement the framework with a keen awareness of the external forces influencing customer behaviour. By combining the insights gained from the JTBD framework with an understanding of economic, cultural, technological, and regulatory contexts, companies can better adapt to changing customer preferences and make more informed strategic decisions.

12 Influence of Bias

The influence of bias is a critical consideration when using the "Jobs To Be Done" (JTBD) framework or any other research methodology. Bias can significantly impact the effectiveness and accuracy of the insights generated through the JTBD framework. Here's a detailed explanation of this limitation:

Researcher Bias: Researcher bias refers to the subjective influence of the researcher's opinions, beliefs, or preconceptions on the research process and findings. In the context of JTBD, it can manifest in several ways:

a. **Selective Observation:** Researchers may unconsciously or consciously focus on information that confirms their existing beliefs or hypotheses, potentially overlooking data that contradicts their assumptions.

b. **Interpretation Bias:** Researchers may interpret customer responses in a way that aligns with their preconceived notions. This can lead to misinterpretation of data or overemphasis on certain insights.

c. **Confirmation Bias:** Researchers may seek out or give more weight to data that confirms their hypotheses about the jobs customers are trying to get done, thereby ignoring or downplaying data that challenges their assumptions.

d. **Cultural Bias:** Researcher bias can extend to cultural bias, where researchers may project their cultural perspectives onto customers from different backgrounds, leading to inaccurate insights.

Participant Bias: Bias is not limited to researchers; it can also affect participants involved in JTBD research. Customers might not always express their true needs and motivations due to social desirability bias, where they provide responses they believe the researcher wants to hear. This can skew the data and lead to inaccurate job descriptions.

Data Collection Bias: The methods used to collect data for JTBD research can introduce bias. For instance, the design of survey questions or the selection of interviewees can inadvertently steer responses in a particular direction, leading to potentially misleading insights.

Cultural and Language Bias: The framework's application in culturally diverse contexts can be challenging. Language and cultural biases can influence the interpretation of customer statements. Translating job descriptions from one language to another might not capture the nuances correctly, leading to bias in the analysis.

Experience Bias: Researchers' and participants' personal experiences can impact their understanding of job descriptions. Individuals may extrapolate their own experiences onto the data, which can limit the framework's ability to uncover diverse job descriptions.

In summary, the influence of bias—both from researchers and participants—can introduce limitations and inaccuracies. Researchers must remain vigilant in addressing bias to ensure the framework's effectiveness in understanding the jobs customers are trying to get done.

In conclusion, while the Jobs to be Done (JTBD) framework can be a powerful tool for identifying customer needs and preferences, it also has several limitations.

Companies need to be aware of these limitations and supplement the JTBD framework with other research methods and techniques to understand their customers and their needs better. By doing so, companies can create products and services that better meet the needs of their customers and stay ahead of the competition in an ever-changing market.

INNOVATION'S HIDDEN WALLS

* * *

2

Limitations of Design Thinking

Design thinking is a problem-solving methodology that emphasizes a human-centered, creative, and iterative approach to finding innovative solutions. It has gained popularity in various industries for its effectiveness in addressing complex challenges and fostering innovation.

Key Principles of Design Thinking:

1. **Human-Centered Design:** Design thinking starts with a deep understanding of the end-users. It focuses on empathizing with their needs, aspirations, and challenges. By putting the human perspective at the forefront, it aims to create solutions that genuinely resonate with users.
2. **Iterative Process:** Design thinking is highly iterative, with an emphasis on continuous prototyping and testing. It encourages a willingness to experiment and learn from failures, leading to refinements and improvements throughout the design process.
3. **Collaboration:** Design thinking is a collaborative effort that involves multidisciplinary teams. It brings together individuals with diverse skills and perspectives to generate a wide range of ideas and approaches.
4. **Creative Problem Solving:** Creativity is central to design thinking. It encourages "thinking outside the box" and leveraging creative techniques like brainstorming, mind mapping, and visualization to explore new

possibilities.

5. **User Empathy:** The methodology emphasizes the importance of under-standing the users' emotional and cognitive needs. Practitioners strive to "walk in the users' shoes" to gain insights into their experiences and challenges.

Stages of Design Thinking:

Design thinking typically follows a series of stages, which may vary in terminology but generally include the following:

1. **Empathize:** In this initial stage, designers seek to understand the users and their needs. This involves conducting interviews, observations, and surveys to gather insights into the users' experiences and pain points.

2. **Define:** After collecting information, designers define the problem to be solved. They distill their findings into clear problem statements or design challenges, ensuring a focused direction for the design process.

3. **Ideate:** Ideation is the creative phase, where multidisciplinary teams brainstorm and generate a wide range of ideas and potential solutions. There are no bad ideas at this stage, and the goal is to encourage creativity and exploration.

4. **Prototype:** Designers create rough, low-cost prototypes of their ideas. These prototypes can be physical models, wireframes, or even sketches. The purpose is to quickly visualize and test concepts.

5. **Test:** In this stage, designers gather user feedback by testing the prototypes with the target audience. The feedback helps identify what works, what doesn't, and where improvements are needed.

6. **Iterate:** Based on the feedback received, designers refine and iterate on their ideas, often cycling back through the stages as necessary. This iterative process continues until a successful solution is developed.

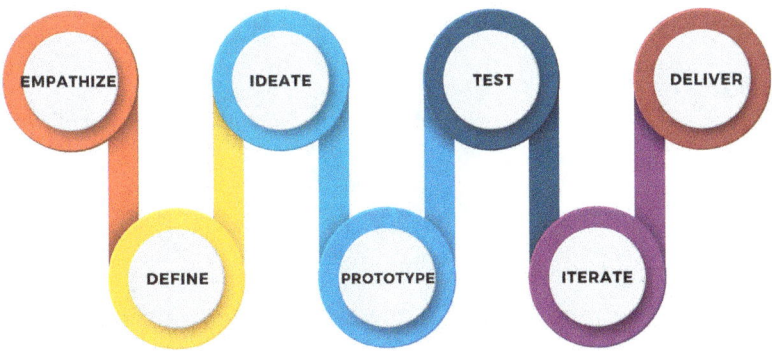

Design thinking is not limited to any specific industry. It has been used in product design, software development, service design, healthcare, education, and more. For example, it has been employed to create user-friendly apps, design patient-centered healthcare experiences, and develop innovative classroom teaching methods.

Design thinking is a powerful methodology that has the potential to address complex problems, spark innovation, and create user-centric solutions. However, like any approach, it also has its limitations, which we'll explore in the next section.

* * *

Limitations of Design Thinking

Design Thinking has become a buzzword in the world of innovation and problem-solving. It's often touted as the key to unlocking creativity, driving growth, and staying ahead of the competition.

But, Is it as good as people say it is? Is it delivering on its promises? Is the excitement justified?

Is Design Thinking really the best tool for innovation?

"Design Thinking: The magic wand that can turn a pile of Post-it notes into a 'breakthrough innovation'... or just a colorful mess."

First, it's important to acknowledge that Design Thinking can be a valuable tool for solving certain types of problems, particularly user-centric ones requiring a deep understanding of customer needs and pain points. However, it's not a panacea. Design Thinking may be less effective when it comes to driving broader business strategy and transformational change.

Nokia's experience is a prime example of how over-reliance on Design Thinking can lead to a company's downfall.

In the early 2000s, Nokia was the undisputed leader in the mobile phone industry, with a reputation for producing high-quality, reliable, and user-friendly phones. The company was renowned for its Design Thinking approach, which emphasized understanding user needs, desires, and pain points to create user-centred products. However, Nokia struggled to keep up when the smartphone revolution took off.

While Nokia's design thinking approach focused on incremental improvements to existing products, Steve Jobs and Apple were busy disrupting the market with their iPods and iPhones. Jobs famously declared that "people don't know what they want until you show it to them" and relied on his intuition to create products that transformed the market. Apple's approach starkly contrasted with Nokia's user-centred approach, which involved extensive user research and testing.

Nokia's Design Thinking approach gave the company sustainable innovation rather than disruptive innovation. While Jobs was working on the App Store for iPhone, Nokia's design thinking approach was working on modifying the buttons and finding the right shape for the button on its mobile phone when the touchscreen was going to enter and rule the world.

This raises the question — why couldn't Nokia's design thinkers come up with disruptive concepts as Apple did?

"Nokia was all about finding the perfect button, but Apple was too busy inventing the 'I-don't-need-buttons' era."

Blackberry, formerly known as Research In Motion (RIM), was once a dominant player in the mobile phone market. The company had a reputation for producing secure and reliable phones that were popular among business professionals. In part, Blackberry's success was attributed to its strong design thinking team and its focus on user-centred design. However, the company's fortunes changed dramatically with the rise of the iPhone and Android smartphones. Despite Blackberry's investment in design thinking, the company failed to keep up with the rapidly changing market.

One of the key reasons behind Blackberry's downfall was its reluctance to adapt to emerging market trends and opportunities. Blackberry's design thinking approach was focused on incremental improvements to its existing product line rather than driving broader business strategy and transformational change. The company was slow to adopt touchscreen technology and failed to anticipate the emergence of app stores and the importance of the developer community. This led to a lack of innovation and differentiation in the company's product line, eventually leading to its demise.

Blackberry's design thinking approach was overly prescriptive and focused on a narrow set of user needs and pain points.

"Blackberry was all about 'staying in touch' but forgot that smartphones were more about 'touch and swipe'!"

01 User Myopia

One of the critical mistakes of the Design Thinking methodology is its myopic focus on existing users rather than exploring new market opportunities.

> *"If Design Thinking were a dating app, it would be called 'Ex-clusive' – only for existing users!"*

Nokia's and Blackberry's approach to design thinking was to observe the same customers repeatedly and make incremental improvements to their existing products. This approach severely limits the potential for disruptive innovation. Businesses that rely solely on design thinking risk falling into the trap of only making minor improvements to existing products rather than pushing the boundaries and creating truly innovative solutions.

Cirque Du Soleil and Southwest Airlines are great examples of businesses that achieved innovation without relying on design thinking. Both companies targeted non-customers rather than existing customers and created entirely new markets.

Caramer Estate — The Australian company Casella Wines is a prime example of a business that fell into the trap of relying on design thinking. When they launched their Value brand Caramer Estate in the USA, they studied the market deeply, spending time with customers, and making changes to their product. However, their solution was incremental, and they failed to differentiate themselves from hundreds of other value brands in the market.

When Casella Wines shifted its focus to non-customers, it launched a new wine called YellowTail that targeted beer and soft drink drinkers. It was a disruptive product, as it was cheaper, with less ritual, and sweeter than other wines on the market.

Olay — In the late 1990s, P&G's Oil of Olay brand struggled to capture the fifty-plus female demographic in the beauty industry. Despite P&G's extensive use of design thinking methodology to understand the needs and preferences of this target market, the brand failed to improve sales growth significantly.

The breakthrough for P&G came when someone within the company went beyond the target segment and identified a new group of women in their mid-thirties who were anxious about the first signs of ageing. This group of women was committed to a rigorous skincare routine, regularly using moisturizers, cleansers, and toners to maintain a youthful and healthy appearance. By understanding the unarticulated needs of this new target segment, P&G was able to redefine its value proposition and create a new product that met its needs.

Design thinking alone would not have solved P&G's reinvention problem. By focusing solely on the existing target market, P&G would have missed the opportunity to identify a new, untapped segment of customers. To truly reinvent the brand and increase sales growth, P&G needed to go beyond design thinking and adopt a more comprehensive approach that included market research, customer insights, and strategic planning.

These examples illustrate that studying the same customers repeatedly can be limiting and unproductive. Businesses that rely solely on design thinking to make incremental improvements risk becoming complacent and failing to identify new market opportunities.

02 The Big Picture

One of the critical flaws in the design thinking approach is that it fails to take a holistic approach. It focuses on a small area and ignores the larger picture, leading to several businesses failing despite relying heavily on design thinking.

"Design Thinking's roadmap: Start with a microbe, zoom in on an ant, and oops, we missed the forest!"

Sony is a perfect example of this. It had a design thinking approach and divisions for electronics, computers, hardware, software, and music. Despite this, the design thinking approach could not bring a product like iPod to the market. On the other hand, Steve Jobs never bothered about design thinking, yet the iPod succeeded.

Some still may argue that the design thinking methodology used by designer Jonathan Ive was the reason behind the iPod's success. Undoubtedly, the iPod device had a superior user interface and file transfer capabilities compared to other devices in the market. Moreover, Steve Jobs asked his team to shift various tasks, such as making song lists, from the device to the personal computer. The introduction of the scroll wheel made it easier to use than other devices available at that time. However, these were just incremental innovations that competitors could easily replicate.

Interestingly, sales were poor when the iPod was first launched despite its wonderful interface and aesthetics. Shouldn't design thinking methodology have ensured the success of the product?

In reality, design thinking takes a narrow approach that stops at the product and users, failing to consider the larger picture. Instead, a holistic approach is needed to succeed in business, as exemplified by Steve Jobs.

Steve Jobs had a visionary approach that went beyond just the product and focused on understanding how customers could obtain songs. He identified that customers did not want to download entire albums and only wanted specific songs without paying for the whole album. With this insight, he created the iTunes Store and sold each song for 99 cents. This proved to be a game-changer as iPod sales picked up.

Yet, iPod sales were not soaring as high as expected. The turning point came when Steve Jobs introduced the iTunes store for Windows. Now, the sales skyrocketed. This shows that a user-centred device design alone cannot guarantee success.

Surprisingly, Apple's design team couldn't come up with the idea for the iTunes Store despite being a company that heavily relied on design thinking. Ironically, the iPod, initially conceptualized by a computer engineer (Tony Fadell), ended up being the product that revolutionized the music industry.

Similarly, it's a wonder why the Design Thinking team at Sony, who owned music labels and had a software division, could not come up with a concept like the iTunes Store and the selling of each song for 99 cents. Despite having all the necessary resources, the design thinking team failed to develop a groundbreaking idea that could revolutionize the music industry. This proves that the design thinking approach is not always the solution to every business problem, and a more holistic approach like Steve Jobs' is necessary to succeed in business.

A holistic approach considering the entire business model and customer experience sets a company apart.

YellowTail and Seeing Beyond Users— Another critical factor that contributed to the success of the YellowTail brand was Casella Wines' ability to leverage the Australian government's advertisement campaign promoting Australian products in the USA during the Sydney Olympics in 2000. The brand cleverly piggybacked on these advertisements, incorporating Australian symbols such as the Wallaby on its packaging and aligning itself with everything Australian. This approach enabled the brand to establish a strong and unique identity in the minds of American consumers, setting it apart from other Australian brands that launched in the USA around the same time.

This idea of using an Australian association to market YellowTail would never come from User Research or any Design Thinking process. It required someone to think holistically and see opportunities beyond the product and user research. The design thinking team of other Australian brands launched then in the USA failed to leverage this opportunity as YellowTail did. This shows that the Design Thinking methodology is not the be-all and end-all of business success. It fails to identify critical factors and opportunities that could give a business an edge over its competitors.

A holistic approach is needed that considers all aspects of the business, including external factors, to succeed truly.

03 User-centred Thinking

User-centred thinking is a core principle of design thinking. It emphasizes understanding and prioritizing the needs, preferences, and experiences of the end-users throughout the design process. This approach is crucial for creating solutions that genuinely resonate with users and address their real-life challenges. However, while user-centered thinking is a strength of design thinking, it can also lead to limitations in certain contexts. Let's explore both aspects:

"When Design Thinking focuses on users, even a coffee cup can become an intergalactic spaceship."

How Design Thinking Focuses on User-Centered Thinking:

1. **Empathetic Research:** Design thinking begins with empathetic research to deeply understand users. This research includes interviews, observations, and surveys to gain insights into users' behaviors, pain points, and aspirations.
2. **Persona Development:** Design thinking often involves creating user personas, which are detailed representations of typical users. These personas guide the design process by ensuring that user needs and preferences remain at the forefront.
3. **Idea Generation:** During the ideation phase, teams use their knowledge of users to brainstorm creative solutions that directly address user needs. This stage encourages diverse thinking and the generation of user-

focused ideas.

4. **Prototyping and Testing:** Prototypes are developed based on user insights, and user testing is a fundamental part of design thinking. These tests involve real users interacting with prototypes to provide feedback and validate the design.

5. **Iterative Improvement:** Design thinking is highly iterative, allowing for continuous refinement of solutions based on user feedback. This ensures that the final product aligns with user expectations.

However, it is important to recognize that user-centred thinking has been integral to successful businesses for centuries before "Design Thinking" was even coined.

For instance, in the 1960s, Sam Walton, the founder of Walmart, built his business around thinking from the user's perspective. He understood customers wanted low prices and convenience and created a business model that offered both. This idea of putting the customer at the centre has made Walmart one of the most successful companies in the world.

Another great example of user-centred thinking comes from Aristide Boucicaut, the founder of Le Bon Marché, the world's first department store, in 1852. Let me repeat — Boucicaut built the departmental store in 1852.

Boucicaut designed every aspect of his store with the customer at the forefront. He introduced price tags, eliminating customers' anxiety while haggling for a fair price. He also eliminated floor stalkers, allowing customers to browse at their own pace. He even provided free entry and allowed customers to browse without buying anything, a revolutionary idea at that time. Boucicaut was also the first to introduce restrooms for women, and he utilized large windows for grand-scale visual merchandising. People would visit his store daily to see the new displays in the front window.

While Boucicaut's ideas may seem basic in the modern era, they were groundbreaking at that time. His customer-centred approach set a new standard for businesses, proving that putting the customer first is essential for success.

Despite this, someone eventually coined the term "Design Thinking" and narrowed the approach to a small area, taking credit for the basic concept that had existed for centuries. While it's important to acknowledge the contribution of design thinking to the business world, it's essential to recognize that user-centred thinking existed long before it was packaged under the label of design thinking. Any successful business model must prioritize the customer experience, a fundamental principle that has existed for centuries.

Limitations Arising from User-Centered Thinking:

1. **Niche Solutions:** Overemphasizing individual user preferences can lead to the development of niche solutions that cater to a specific group but may not have broad market appeal.
2. **Resource and Time Constraints:** The comprehensive user research, prototyping, and testing involved in user-centered thinking can be resource-intensive and time-consuming, making it challenging in situations with limited resources or tight deadlines.
3. **Balancing Conflicting User Needs:** Users within a target audience may have conflicting needs or preferences, making it difficult to design a one-size-fits-all solution.
4. **Innovation vs. User Expectations:** A strong focus on meeting user expectations may limit the pursuit of groundbreaking, disruptive innovations that users may not have explicitly expressed.
5. **Overlooking Broader Organizational Goals:** A hyper-focus on users may lead Design Thinking teams to prioritize user needs and preferences over broader organizational goals. While user-centric design is crucial, it should align with the strategic objectives and sustainability of the organization. In some cases, an exclusive focus on users can lead to solutions that are misaligned with the company's long-term vision.
6. **Neglecting Technological or Market Feasibility:** User-centered design primarily emphasizes what users want and need. However, it may not take into account technological feasibility or market viability. A solution that perfectly meets user needs might not be feasible to implement from

a technical or financial perspective. This can lead to the development of concepts that are impractical or unsustainable.

7. **Ignoring Regulatory or Ethical Constraints:** Design Thinking often revolves around creative problem-solving, which can sometimes overlook regulatory or ethical constraints. An obsession with user satisfaction may result in solutions that inadvertently violate laws or ethical standards, leading to legal issues or public relations problems.

8. **Resistance to Change:** Users may resist change even if it's in their long-term interest. A user-centered approach may inadvertently discourage experimentation and risk-taking because users are accustomed to existing products or processes. This resistance to change can hinder innovation and improvement.

9. **Insufficient Consideration of Industry Trends:** Relying solely on user feedback may cause Design Thinking teams to miss out on emerging industry trends or technological advancements. While it's important to meet current user needs, it's equally crucial to anticipate and adapt to future trends to stay competitive.

10. **Competitive Blind Spots:** A myopic focus on existing users may result in neglecting the broader competitive landscape. Organizations need to be aware of what competitors are doing and consider strategies beyond just satisfying their current users.

Balancing the user-centered approach with considerations for feasibility, constraints, and future trends is essential to overcome these limitations and ensure the long-term success of Design Thinking initiatives.

A Few Examples—

1. **The Ford Edsel:** In the late 1950s, Ford Motor Company introduced the Edsel, a car designed based on extensive user research and market surveys. The company focused intensely on what users wanted at the time. However, the Edsel was a monumental failure, largely due to an overemphasis on users' current preferences, rather than anticipating

future trends. The car had features users said they wanted, but it was too expensive and didn't align with changing consumer tastes.

2. **Google Glass:** Google Glass was hailed as a revolutionary product with a strong user-centered design approach. It aimed to provide users with a hands-free, augmented reality experience. However, it failed to gain traction in the consumer market. This failure was attributed to the fact that Google overemphasized user convenience, neglecting privacy concerns and societal acceptance. It ultimately targeted the wrong user segment and didn't consider the broader social implications.

3. **Microsoft's Clippy:** Microsoft's Clippy, the animated paperclip assistant in Microsoft Office, was a user-centered design effort to enhance user productivity. However, it became one of the most infamous software features ever. Users found it intrusive and annoying, leading to widespread criticism. The failure of Clippy demonstrated that an exclusive focus on users' needs without considering user feedback can result in frustration.

4. **New Coke:** In 1985, Coca-Cola introduced "New Coke" after extensive user research indicated that users preferred a sweeter taste. However, this change failed to resonate with consumers, who had a strong emotional attachment to the original formula. The user-centered approach led to a significant backlash, and Coca-Cola had to reintroduce the original formula as "Coca-Cola Classic."

5. **Amazon Fire Phone:** Amazon's Fire Phone was designed with a user-focused approach to create a seamless shopping experience. While it included features users asked for, such as 3D technology, it ultimately flopped in the market. The phone didn't gain user acceptance, partly because it was too closely tied to Amazon's ecosystem and had limited third-party app support. This showed that an exclusive focus on user convenience can lead to tunnel vision and missed opportunities.

These examples highlight the importance of balancing user-centered design with considerations for broader societal trends, future market conditions, and the competitive landscape. User feedback is crucial, but it should be incorporated into a holistic design process that takes into account multiple factors for long-term success.

04 Cognitive Biases in User Research

User research is the bedrock of design thinking, providing critical insights into users' needs, behaviours, and pain points. It fuels the empathetic understanding that design thinking champions. This research delves deep into the users' experiences and challenges, forming the foundation for identifying their needs and concerns.

This reliance on user research positions design thinking as a potent approach to crafting user-centric and innovative solutions. It ensures that design decisions are rooted in tangible user insights, ultimately resulting in products and services that better align with user expectations.

However, the same user research that design thinking leans on can paradoxically lead to the failure of design thinking solutions due to the presence of cognitive biases. Cognitive biases are systematic patterns of deviation from rational judgment, often arising from information processing shortcuts. In user research within design thinking, these biases can significantly affect how researchers interpret and act on data gathered from users.

"User research: uncovering what users say they do. Cognitive biases: revealing what users actually do when they think no one's watching."

Examples of a few Cognitive Biases in User Research:

1. **Confirmation Bias:** This bias unfolds when researchers unconsciously seek, interpret, and recall information that confirms their preexisting beliefs or hypotheses. In the realm of design thinking, confirmation bias

can manifest as a selective focus on user feedback that aligns with the team's initial assumptions. In doing so, it may potentially lead to the dismissal of contradictory insights that challenge these assumptions.

2. **Recency Bias:** Researchers may be unduly influenced by the most recent user feedback, disproportionately emphasizing the significance of the latest data collected. In the process, earlier, equally valuable insights may be overlooked or underappreciated, potentially skewing the overall picture.

3. **Availability Heuristic:** This bias involves the overestimation of the importance of information that is readily available or easily recalled. In user research, it may manifest as giving more weight to vivid or memorable user experiences, while downplaying less striking but still relevant data.

4. **Anchoring Bias:** Anchoring bias emerges when researchers assign excessive weight to the first piece of information they receive. In the context of user research, the initial user feedback often sets the tone for the entire project. As a result, there's a risk of limiting exploration into alternative viewpoints and missing out on a broader spectrum of insights.

The presence of cognitive biases in design thinking research underscores the critical need for self-awareness and robust methodologies within design teams. To harness the full potential of user research while evading the pitfalls of cognitive bias, teams should actively implement strategies such as blind analysis, peer review, diversified data sources, and longitudinal studies.

Yet, it's crucial to acknowledge that the field of cognitive biases is intricate and multifaceted. Even designers, who pride themselves on their ability to identify and understand user biases during research, may not be fully cognizant of the biases they themselves hold. Cognitive biases can manifest in subtle and intricate ways, and designers, like anyone else, can be susceptible to their effects. In certain contexts, or due to their own confirmation bias, designers might unconsciously alter their behaviour or misinterpret elements of their research.

Even experts in psychology and neurobiology do not claim comprehensive insight into the biases of others; this is a specialized field that requires in-depth training beyond the typical designer's education. Despite this, it is not uncommon to find designers confidently asserting their proficiency in identifying and neutralizing user biases. This overconfidence sometimes exposes a superficial grasp of the complexities of cognitive biases and can ironically lead to more biased research outcomes.

Furthermore, the concept of self-awareness, while valuable, is not always attainable in its fullest sense. Designers, like any individuals, can sometimes display egoistic attitudes, indicating a lack of self-awareness. The reality is that designers are also human beings, and they, too, are susceptible to cognitive biases. Thus, identifying and understanding user biases during research can be challenging when designers themselves may not be entirely self-aware of their own biases.

Recognizing and comprehending user cognitive biases is undoubtedly crucial for crafting effective design solutions. However, it is equally vital to acknowledge that biases are pervasive, not only in users but also within designers themselves. In this intricate landscape, self-awareness and humility can serve as valuable allies in the pursuit of unbiased and user-centric design thinking.

05 Empathy

Design thinking places a significant and commendable emphasis on empathy as a core principle. It recognizes the importance of understanding and resonating with the feelings, needs, and perspectives of the end-users. While this focus on empathy is a vital aspect of creating user-centric solutions, it can also present limitations and challenges within the design thinking process.

Empathy drives designers to step into the shoes of the end-users, fostering a deep understanding of their experiences, challenges, and aspirations. Empathy helps in framing design challenges accurately from the user's viewpoint. It ensures that the problems being addressed are genuinely user-centric, which is crucial for effective problem-solving. By empathizing with users, designers gain valuable insights that fuel creative ideation. It allows teams to brainstorm innovative solutions that directly address user needs and pain points. Empathy guides the design of prototypes that resonate with users, as they are informed by the emotional and practical aspects of the user experience.

"Empathy in design thinking is like trying to read a novel in a foreign language while wearing someone else's glasses – things might get lost in translation."

Limitations and Challenges of Overemphasizing Empathy:

1. **Bias Towards Familiarity:** Overemphasizing empathy may lead to a bias toward designing solutions that closely resemble familiar user experiences. Designers, by immersing themselves deeply in the user's world, might develop a strong attachment to the status quo. This can hinder exploration of innovative solutions that deviate from established norms. As a result, there may be a missed opportunity for groundbreaking design.

2. **Subjectiveness:** Design Thinking methodology often promotes a type of empathy that involves putting oneself in the shoes of the user and experiencing their needs and wants firsthand. This can be problematic, as it assumes that designers can fully understand the perspectives and experiences of others, which is often not the case. It is important to recognize that empathy can be subjective and influenced by personal biases and experiences. Empathy involves understanding and sharing the feelings of another person. However, every person's experiences are unique, shaped by their past experiences, upbringing, biology, and many other factors. This means that it is often difficult, if not impossible, to empathize with someone else's experiences truly.

3. **Empathy Burnout:** Constantly immersing in the user's world, especially if it involves emotionally charged or challenging scenarios, can lead to empathy burnout among designers. Empathy burnout is akin to emotional fatigue and can impact the quality of design work. Designers may find it challenging to continue empathizing effectively and may become desensitized to user experiences over time.

4. **Overpersonalization:** Designers, in their quest to empathize deeply, may overpersonalize solutions based on the specific experiences and needs of a particular user or user group. This can lead to the creation of products or services that are excessively tailored to the idiosyncrasies of a niche audience. While such solutions might address the unique needs of a few, they often lack broader market appeal and could struggle with scalability.

5. **Limited Objectivity:** Overemphasizing empathy can make it challenging for designers to maintain objectivity. They may become emotionally invested in certain solutions, which can lead to a lack of critical evaluation and a reluctance to consider alternative viewpoints or ideas. Objectivity is crucial in the design process to ensure that the best possible solutions are pursued, irrespective of personal biases.

6. **Potential Misalignment with Business Goals:** While empathy ensures user satisfaction and alignment with user needs, it may not always align seamlessly with broader business objectives or feasibility. Designers may need to reconcile user empathy with the practical aspects of implementing solutions, considering factors like cost, resources, and profitability. Striking a balance between empathy and business viability can be a complex endeavor.

7. **Resource and Time Constraints:** Achieving deep empathy often requires extended periods of user research and engagement. In resource-constrained or time-sensitive projects, dedicating significant resources to empathetic research may not be practical. This can create a tension between the desire for deep empathy and the reality of project constraints.

8. **Lack of Broader Information:** There are limitations to the amount of empathy that can be developed through research and observation

alone. Designers may not have access to all the information needed to understand the experiences of their users fully. This can lead to incomplete or inaccurate assumptions about user needs and behaviours, resulting in ineffective or inappropriate solutions.

Given these complexities, it is nearly impossible for someone to understand and share another person's feelings completely, especially when the experiences differ vastly from their own.

06 Ignorance of Organizational Culture

A brand's success doesn't solely hinge on its products or services; the health of its organizational culture plays an equally vital role. Design thinking teams, while often seen as providers of innovative business strategies, can sometimes overlook the significance of fostering a supportive organizational culture. Without such a culture, even the most ingenious ideas can falter.

Regrettably, many design thinking teams lack a comprehensive understanding of how to establish and sustain a robust organizational culture. Essential factors like psychological safety, the impact of radical transparency, and strategies for enhancing work engagement often elude their grasp. Instead, they may focus primarily on idea generation without giving due consideration to the practicalities of implementation. As a result, their solutions can appear half-baked and impractical.

"Organizational culture is like a recipe book in the kitchen of innovation. Design thinkers sometimes focus so much on the ingredients that they forget the oven is broken."

Organizational culture constitutes a tapestry of shared values, beliefs, behaviors, and norms that define a company's modus operandi. It weaves its influence into decision-making, communication, innovation, and the broader spectrum of business practices. The failure to recognize and integrate this cultural element can give rise to multiple limitations within the design thinking process:

1. Resistance to Change: The prevailing organizational culture frequently mirrors a company's historical practices and traditional ways of doing things. When design thinking initiatives are introduced without a regard for this existing culture, resistance from employees accustomed to the status quo often ensues. Such changes may be perceived as disruptive and met with reluctance.

2. Misalignment with Core Values: Design thinking projects that do not harmonize with the organization's fundamental values and mission can generate conflicts. If the solutions proposed through design thinking run counter to the company's principles, it can lead to a lack of buy-in from both leadership and employees.

3. Inadequate Support: Design thinking thrives on cross-functional collaboration and necessitates support from diverse departments. Neglecting the influence of organizational culture may result in inadequate support from key stakeholders who may not be in alignment with the design thinking approach. This lack of support can impede the successful execution of design projects.

4. Cultural Barriers to Creativity: Certain organizational cultures might not encourage or endorse creativity and innovation. Design thinking, with its pronounced emphasis on ideation and creative problem-solving, can face considerable obstacles when it clashes with a culture that places a premium on conformity and stability.

5. Lack of Psychological Safety: To realize its potential, design thinking relies on the cultivation of a culture of psychological safety. In such an environment, team members should feel at ease sharing ideas, taking calculated risks, and challenging established norms. The failure to account for this cultural facet can stifle the open exchange of ideas and impede the design thinking process.

By neglecting this foundational aspect of a prosperous business, design-thinking teams unwittingly set themselves up for potential failure. To leverage the full potential of design thinking, it is imperative to strike a harmonious balance between innovative thinking and a culture that supports, encourages, and integrates it.

07 Limited Scalability

Design Thinking principles work remarkably well in smaller, agile teams where direct engagement with end-users is feasible and decision-making is decentralized. However, as projects and organizations scale up, design thinking can face substantial challenges.

"Scaling design thinking is like teaching a dog new tricks. It's charming at home, but when you try it in the park, it's chaos."

Challenges in Scaling Design Thinking:

1. **Resource Intensity:** Design thinking demands significant resources, including time, skilled personnel, and user research capabilities. In larger organizations, managing these resources across multiple teams and projects can become complex and resource-intensive.
2. **Coordination and Communication:** As projects scale, ensuring effective coordination and communication among various teams and stakeholders becomes a challenge. The free flow of information and insights, which is pivotal in design thinking, can become disrupted in larger, more hierarchical organizations.
3. **Alignment with Organizational Goals:** Scaling design thinking can create a misalignment with organizational goals and strategies. Larger organizations often have multiple departments and initiatives, and

ensuring that design thinking aligns with these diverse agendas can be difficult.

4. **Cultural Barriers:** Organizations, especially larger ones, may have ingrained cultures that are resistant to change. Design thinking's focus on iterative experimentation can clash with cultures that value stability and consistency.

5. **Complex Decision-Making Structures:** In larger organizations, decision-making structures are often more complex, involving multiple layers of management. This can slow down the iterative nature of design thinking and hinder its responsiveness.

6. **Standardization and Repetition:** Larger projects often require standardized processes and repeated actions to maintain consistency. Design thinking, with its fluid and adaptive nature, can struggle in such environments.

The challenges of resource allocation, coordination, alignment, and cultural adaptation must be thoughtfully addressed to ensure the successful scalability of design thinking.

Here are some cases where design thinking's iterative approach may be time-consuming and impractical on a larger scale:

1. **Large-Scale Infrastructure Projects:** Design thinking's iterative approach, which involves empathizing with end-users and prototyping solutions, may not be feasible for massive infrastructure projects like building highways, bridges, or airports. These projects often have strict timelines and budget constraints, making it impractical to engage in lengthy iterations.

2. **Emergency Response:** In emergency response scenarios, such as natural disasters or public health crises, rapid decision-making and execution are critical. While design thinking's user-centric approach is valuable, there might not be sufficient time for extensive user research and iterative prototyping when immediate actions are required.

3. **Military Operations:** Military operations involve complex planning, coordination, and execution. Design thinking's iterative process may not align with the urgency and precision required in military scenarios. Rapid decision-making and adherence to established protocols take precedence over user-centered design in such cases.

4. **Manufacturing and Production Lines:** In manufacturing industries, the production process often follows standardized procedures and requires minimal deviations to maintain efficiency and quality control. Implementing design thinking's iterative approach on a large scale can disrupt established production lines, leading to delays and increased costs.

5. **Government Policies and Regulations:** When governments develop policies, regulations, and laws, they typically involve a thorough legislative process that may not allow for the frequent iterations that design thinking suggests. Policy-making is often influenced by various stakeholders and political considerations, making quick, user-centric iterations challenging.

6. **Large-Scale Data Analysis and Research Studies:** In research and data analysis on a massive scale, such as national surveys or epidemiological studies, the collection and analysis of data follow established protocols to maintain consistency and data integrity. Frequent iterations in research design can compromise the reliability and validity of the findings.

7. **Aerospace and Space Exploration:** Projects in the aerospace and space exploration industries require meticulous planning and adherence to rigorous standards. The iterative nature of design thinking may not align with the precision and safety requirements in these sectors.

8. **Pharmaceutical Drug Development:** The process of developing pharmaceutical drugs is highly regulated and involves extensive clinical trials and safety testing. Frequent iterations in drug development may delay the release of potentially life-saving medications, making design thinking less practical in this context.

These cases emphasize that while design thinking is a valuable problem-solving approach, its iterative nature may not always align with the urgency, precision, and standardization required in specific large-scale industries and projects. In such scenarios, a more linear and established approach is often preferred to ensure efficient execution and safety.

08 Lack of Analytical Depth

Analytical rigour refers to the systematic and meticulous examination, evaluation, and interpretation of data, information, and evidence. It involves critical thinking, logic, and the application of rigorous methods to derive meaningful insights and conclusions. In contrast, design thinking often places a stronger emphasis on creativity, intuition, and empathetic understanding.

The criticism that design thinking lacks analytical depth stems from several key points:

1. **Subjectivity:** Design thinking is often perceived as subjective, relying on individual and team perspectives rather than objective and data-driven analysis. The user-centred approach, while valuable for understanding user needs, can be seen as insufficient for robust problem analysis.

2. **User-Centered Focus:** While the user-centered approach is a core strength of design thinking, it can sometimes lead to overemphasizing user perspectives to the detriment of broader analytical considerations. This focus on users is essential but must be balanced with other data sources.

3. **Emphasis on Ideation:** Design thinking places significant importance on ideation and brainstorming. While this fosters creative thinking, critics argue that it might not provide a structured approach to thoroughly analyze problems and potential solutions.

4. **Limited Quantitative Analysis:** Design thinking tends to utilize qualitative data and insights from user research. Critics contend that the lack of quantitative analysis and data-driven decision-making can lead to biased or inaccurate conclusions.

5. **Ambiguity in Outcomes:** Design thinking often encourages open-ended exploration, which can result in ambiguous outcomes. Critics argue that this ambiguity may hinder precise problem definition and solution evaluation.

6. **Time Constraints:** Design thinking often operates within tight timelines, emphasizing quick ideation and prototyping. While this rapid approach fosters creativity, it may not allow for comprehensive data collection and in-depth analysis, limiting the depth of insight.

7. **Resource Limitations:** Design thinking teams may face resource constraints, including a lack of data analytics expertise. In data-driven projects, the absence of the right resources can hinder the depth of analysis required for complex decisions.

8. **Lack of Statistical Methods:** Design thinking lacks the statistical methods and modeling techniques integral to data-driven approaches, which can limit its analytical depth in specific contexts.

Design thinking can be a valuable tool in the problem-solving toolkit, but it becomes more effective when combined with rigorous analysis in appropriate contexts. The challenge is finding the right balance between creativity and analysis for each unique problem and project.

Sample Scenarios Requiring a Data-Driven Approach

In complex, data-heavy projects, a data-driven approach becomes essential to derive meaningful insights, make informed decisions, and achieve specific outcomes. Design thinking, with its human-centered and creative problem-solving focus, may fall short in such scenarios. Here are some scenarios where a more data-driven approach is necessary:

Healthcare Analytics: When analyzing healthcare data to improve patient outcomes, data-driven analytics are critical. Design thinking may not provide the analytical rigor required to identify patterns, predict disease trends, or optimize treatment protocols.

Example: In healthcare, data-driven analytics are used to predict patient readmission rates based on historical data, enabling hospitals to allocate resources more efficiently. Design thinking alone cannot achieve this level of predictive accuracy.

Financial Forecasting: Financial institutions rely heavily on quantitative analysis to make investment decisions, predict market trends, and manage risk. Design thinking may lack the quantitative depth needed for these critical financial operations.

Example: In stock market analysis, algorithms and statistical models are used to predict stock price movements based on historical data. Design thinking's qualitative approach cannot replace these quantitative methods.

Supply Chain Optimization: Large-scale supply chain management involves vast amounts of data related to inventory, logistics, and demand forecasting. Data-driven approaches are indispensable for optimizing supply chain operations.

Example: Retail companies use data-driven analysis to optimize inventory levels, minimize carrying costs, and enhance product availability. Design thinking may not offer the level of detail required for these data-intensive decisions.

Predictive Maintenance in Manufacturing: Manufacturing plants rely on data analytics to predict equipment failures and schedule maintenance. A data-driven approach is vital for minimizing downtime and production interruptions.

Example: Predictive maintenance uses sensors and machine learning to analyze equipment performance data and predict when machines require maintenance. Design thinking lacks the quantitative sophistication needed for such predictive analysis.

Market Research and Consumer Insights: Understanding consumer behavior and preferences often involves analyzing vast datasets. Data-driven market research tools and techniques provide insights that go beyond what design thinking can uncover.

Example: E-commerce companies use data analytics to segment customers based on their purchase history and browsing behavior. This level of customer segmentation and analysis goes beyond the scope of design thinking.

In summary, the choice between design thinking and a data-driven approach depends on the nature of the project, its goals, and the availability of data. While design thinking is invaluable for fostering creativity and empathy, data-driven approaches are essential when dealing with complex, data-intensive projects where quantitative analysis and predictive modeling are prerequisites for success.

09 Research Methodologies

Time and Money — The design thinking methodology stresses the importance of studying users in depth to understand the needs and preferences of the target market. However, one of the critical drawbacks of this approach is the amount of time and money spent on user research, which can be prohibitively expensive.

Studying existing customers in-depth can result in incremental innovations, but it may not be enough to keep a business ahead of the curve in a rapidly changing market.

Furthermore, extensive user research may not always be the best use of time and resources. While it's essential to understand the needs and preferences of the target market, there is a risk of spending too much time and money on research without making significant progress towards a viable product or service.

"Design thinking can sometimes feel like preparing a gourmet meal when you only needed a quick snack. Bon appétit to your budget!"

Qualitative Research — Many design thinking methodologies rely heavily on qualitative research, which can be biased and subjective and lack statistical significance. Qualitative research methods such as ethnography, in-depth interviews, and focus groups rely heavily on interpretation and subjective analysis, which can result in biased results. Additionally, these methodologies often prioritize the views and opinions of a small sample of users over the larger market trends and data. As a result, the solutions derived from these research methodologies may not be scalable or effective in addressing the needs of the broader market. Furthermore, some design thinking methodologies may not take into account the cultural and social contexts in which the business operates, leading to solutions that are not appropriate or effective in different regions or cultures.

Moreover, qualitative research may not always provide actionable and measurable outcomes, making it difficult for companies to implement the findings into their business strategies.

Another issue with qualitative research is that it can be difficult to replicate or generalize findings to different contexts. This limits the ability to apply the research to other situations or settings, making it less useful for designing solutions that are scalable or have broader applications.

"Design thinking and qualitative research - because sometimes, it's more about opinions than precision!"

Observational Research — Observational research, a common methodology used in design thinking, also has limitations. The main issue with observational research is that it can be biased and subjective based on the researcher's interpretation of what they observe. The researcher may observe only those behaviours that align with their assumptions about the users and ignore other behaviours that may contradict them. This can lead to a limited understanding of the user's needs and behaviours and may not provide a complete picture of the user's experiences.

Additionally, observational research may not capture the context and environment in which the user interacts with the product or service. Observing users in a controlled setting may not reflect the reality of their everyday experiences, which can impact the accuracy of the findings.

Moreover, observational research is time-consuming and resource-intensive, requiring significant money and time investments. This can be a challenge for small businesses or startups that may not have the necessary resources to invest in long-term research projects.

Another limitation of observational research is the small sample size. The insights gathered from this small sample may not necessarily represent the needs and preferences of the larger population.

Other research methodologies used in design thinking include surveys, interviews, and focus groups. The quality of questions and response bias can limit surveys. Interviews can be influenced by the interviewer's biases and limited by the sample size and representativeness. Focus groups can suffer from group dynamics, where participants can influence each other's opinions and limit the range of ideas generated.

"Observational research: where the truth is in the eye of the beholder, but sometimes, the eye needs glasses."

10 Iteration and Prototyping

Iteration and prototyping are foundational to the design thinking methodology, enabling designers to refine their ideas and create superior end products or processes. Through iteration, designers can rapidly produce and evaluate multiple versions, incorporating feedback and learning from failures with each cycle. This process enhances the quality of the final outcome.

Prototyping and iteration also play a vital role in identifying and addressing potential issues in the design process, effectively mitigating the risk of costly errors in the final product. However, it's essential to acknowledge that these practices are not without challenges and limitations.

Time and Cost Constraints: Iteration can be a time-consuming and expensive process, especially when multiple cycles are necessary to arrive at a satisfactory solution. Small businesses and resource-constrained projects may find this aspect of design thinking prohibitive.

Overemphasis on Immediate Results: While iteration is crucial, it can sometimes lead to a "design trap" where designers become too focused on incremental improvements without making significant progress toward a solution. This overemphasis on iteration can detract from long-term planning and strategy.

Resistance to Change: Becoming too attached to a particular design or idea can lead to resistance to change or the exploration of new ideas. This can stifle innovation and hinder a company's ability to adapt to evolving market conditions and customer needs.

Resource and Time Wastage: Iterating multiple times can consume valuable resources and time. It's essential to strike a balance between iteration and other critical aspects of the design process.

False Sense of Progress: A strong focus on prototyping and iteration may give the team a false sense of progress if improvements are not significant. It's important to ensure that iterations lead to meaningful advancements.

Bias Toward Incremental Improvements: An excessive focus on iteration may result in a bias toward incremental improvements rather than innovative, transformative solutions. Design thinking should encourage bold, outside-the-box thinking.

Solution-Centric Approach: The emphasis on prototyping and iteration can sometimes overshadow the crucial phase of problem analysis and definition. It's essential to strike a balance between these aspects of the design process.

User Fatigue: In user-centered design, repeated feedback and testing can lead to user fatigue, potentially diminishing the quality of their insights. Selective and strategic user involvement is key.

Prototyping Excess: The practice of creating numerous prototypes, sometimes exceeding a hundred versions, may not be the most efficient approach. It's vital to address specifications and constraints comprehensively during the concept and design stages to avoid wasteful iterations.

In today's fast-paced world, where technology advances quickly, design thinking should evolve beyond iteration and prototyping to address these limitations effectively. A balanced approach that considers time, cost, long-term strategy, and problem analysis is necessary for the continued success of design thinking.

"Sometimes, design thinking feels like trying to fix a leaky faucet with endless iterations of different-sized wrenches."

"Designers in constant iteration mode are a bit like hamsters on a wheel - they're moving, but they're not getting anywhere new."

11 Customer Journey Mapping

Customer journey mapping is a visual representation of the end-to-end experience a customer has with a product, service, or brand. It provides a detailed view of the customer's interactions, emotions, and touchpoints at various stages, from initial awareness to post-purchase support.

In the context of design thinking, customer journey mapping is a vital tool used to gain a deep understanding of the user's experience. Design thinkers employ this technique to empathize with the customer, identify pain points, and uncover opportunities for improvement.

Design thinkers create a visual representation of the customer's journey, mapping each touchpoint and interaction. This often includes the user's emotional state, needs, and goals at each stage. Once the journey map is complete, design thinkers use it as a reference point for brainstorming solutions and innovations. They identify areas for improvement and ideate on ways to enhance the user experience.

Though Customer Journey Mapping is a valuable methodology, there are limitations to this approach. Below, we explore the potential drawbacks and challenges associated with it:

1. Simplification of Complex Journeys: Customer journey maps aim to simplify the customer experience to make it more understandable and actionable. However, in doing so, they may oversimplify the intricate and multifaceted nature of customer journeys. Real-life customer experiences can be highly complex, with multiple touchpoints, emotions, and decision-making processes. Customer journey maps may struggle to capture the full complexity of these journeys.

2. Subjectivity and Assumptions: Creating a customer journey map often involves making assumptions and subjective interpretations of the customer's experience. Designers rely on available data, user feedback, and their own insights to construct the map. As a result, the map may not always accurately represent the diverse perspectives and emotions of all customers.

3. Lack of Real-time Insights: Customer journey mapping typically relies on historical or static data, making it challenging to incorporate real-time insights into the map. Customer experiences can change rapidly due to external factors, market dynamics, or technological advancements. A static customer journey map may become outdated quickly.

4. Incomplete Data: Customer journey maps are only as reliable as the data and insights used to create them. Incomplete or inaccurate data can lead to biased or flawed maps that do not reflect the true customer experience.

5. Difficulty in Capturing Emotional Aspects: Emotions play a significant role in the customer journey, influencing decisions, satisfaction, and loyalty. However, customer journey maps may struggle to capture the emotional aspects of the journey effectively. Designers may need to rely on indirect indicators or surveys, which may not fully reveal the emotional nuances.

6. Lack of Contextual Understanding: Customer journey maps may not provide a holistic view of the customer's life or broader context. Understanding the customer's lifestyle, preferences, and external influences is crucial for creating truly user-centric solutions. Customer journey maps may not delve deeply into these contextual aspects.

7. Overemphasis on Touchpoints: Customer journey maps often focus on touchpoints or interactions with the company, but they may overlook the broader context in which these interactions occur. Understanding the customer's full context can provide richer insights into their needs and motivations.

8. Rigidity and Linearity: Traditional customer journey maps tend to present the customer's journey as a linear sequence of steps. In reality, customer journeys can be non-linear and dynamic, with customers moving back and forth between stages or touchpoints. This rigidity can limit the map's accuracy.

9. Lack of Cultural Sensitivity: Customer journey maps may not always account for cultural variations, which can significantly impact the customer's experience and expectations. Designers need to consider cultural nuances to create solutions that resonate with diverse audiences.

While customer journey mapping is a valuable tool, designers should be aware of these limitations and use them as a complement to other research and design techniques. A more comprehensive and nuanced understanding of the customer's experience can be achieved by combining customer journey mapping with user research, usability testing, and contextual inquiry.

"The customer journey map: where 'You are here' is always clear, but 'Where you should be going' remains a mystery."

12 Lack of Diversity of Ideas

The design thinking methodology is celebrated for its emphasis on collaboration, creativity, and innovation. However, one of the limitations is the potential for a lack of diversity in the generation of ideas. Here's a detailed exploration of this limitation:

1. Groupthink and Conformity: In design thinking, teams often collaborate to brainstorm ideas and solutions. While collaboration is beneficial, it can sometimes lead to groupthink and conformity. Group members may conform to dominant ideas or the perceived consensus, stifling the diversity of thought. This can hinder the generation of truly innovative or unconventional solutions.

2. Dominance of Vocal Voices: Within design thinking teams, some individuals may be more vocal and assertive than others. Their ideas may receive more attention and consideration, potentially overshadowing the contributions of quieter team members. This dominance can limit the range of ideas considered during the ideation process.

3. Homogeneous Teams: The composition of design thinking teams can impact the diversity of ideas generated. Homogeneous teams with similar backgrounds, experiences, and perspectives may produce ideas that reflect a limited range of viewpoints. This can lead to a lack of diversity in the generated solutions.

4. Time and Resource Constraints: Design thinking sessions are often conducted within a defined timeframe. This time constraint can limit the depth and breadth of idea generation, as teams may not have sufficient time to explore a wide range of possibilities.

5. Fear of Criticism: Team members may be reluctant to propose unconventional or risky ideas due to a fear of criticism or rejection. This fear can lead to self-censorship and a preference for safe, conservative ideas, limiting the diversity of solutions.

6. Limited Exposure to Diverse Perspectives: Design thinking teams may have limited exposure to diverse perspectives or experiences. This can be particularly challenging when solving problems that involve users from diverse cultural backgrounds or demographics. Without a deep understanding of these diverse perspectives, the generated ideas may lack diversity.

7. Overreliance on Established Ideation Techniques: Design thinking often incorporates established ideation techniques and brainstorming methods. While these techniques are valuable, they can become repetitive, leading to a recycling of familiar ideas rather than the exploration of new and unconventional solutions.

8. Lack of Diverse User Involvement: Design thinking encourages user-centricity, but the diversity of users involved in the process can vary. If user representation is limited to a narrow demographic or excludes underrepresented groups, the generated ideas may not fully address the needs and preferences of a diverse user base.

This lack of diversity in ideas can lead to a narrow focus on specific solutions or ideas, ultimately limiting the potential success of the designed product or service. This problem is exacerbated by the fact that design thinking methodology often prioritizes speed and efficiency, which can result in a rush to settle on the first viable solution rather than exploring all potential options.

"When you put a bunch of identical puzzle pieces together, you don't get a new picture. You just get the same piece over and over again!"

13 Group Brainstorming

Design thinking promotes group brainstorming as a collaborative approach to ideation and problem-solving, recognizing its potential to generate a wealth of creative solutions. However, it's crucial to acknowledge that group brainstorming comes with inherent limitations, especially when viewed in comparison to individual brainstorming or when it's the sole method employed within the design thinking process. Here, we'll explore these potential drawbacks, shedding light on the challenges and constraints faced by design thinkers.

1. Group Dynamics and the Conformity Challenge: Group brainstorming is influenced by various group dynamics, such as the pressure to conform and the desire for consensus. While collaboration is a strength, these dynamics can inadvertently suppress unconventional or divergent ideas. The fear of deviating from the majority's viewpoint or proposing risky concepts may lead to a filtering of ideas. In such scenarios, the full creative potential of each individual may not be realized.

2. Unequal Participation: Participation inequality is a common occurrence in group brainstorming sessions. Some individuals may dominate discussions, monopolizing the idea-generation process, while others remain passive observers. This imbalance can result in the underutilization of team members' diverse perspectives and creative capabilities, limiting the range of ideas produced.

3. Delayed Idea Evaluation: Group brainstorming primarily focuses on idea generation, while the evaluation and selection of ideas often occur after the brainstorming session. The delay in evaluating ideas can lead to the accumulation of numerous unprocessed suggestions, making the subsequent selection process overwhelming and time-consuming.

4. Social Inhibition and Fear of Evaluation: The fear of being judged or evaluated by others, known as evaluation apprehension, can deter individuals from sharing unconventional or untested ideas during group brainstorming. In a design thinking context, this apprehension can stifle the diversity of ideas, as participants may opt for safer, more conventional suggestions to avoid potential criticism or scrutiny.

5. Lack of Reflection and Deep Thinking: Group brainstorming typically emphasizes rapid idea generation. However, this pace may not always allow for deep reflection or the exploration of complex, nuanced concepts. The process can become overly focused on the quantity of ideas rather than their quality, potentially limiting the development of more thoughtful and groundbreaking solutions.

6. The "Design Trap" and Overemphasis on Iteration: The iterative nature of design thinking encourages constant refinement and enhancement of ideas. However, an overemphasis on iteration can lead to a design trap, where the focus on continuous refinement becomes an end in itself rather than a means to a well-defined solution. This can result in a lack of focus on long-term planning and strategy, ultimately impeding progress.

7. The Need for Silent Brainstorming: Group brainstorming is typically a verbal and interactive process. However, introverted individuals or those who prefer silent brainstorming may feel their voices drowned out. Silent brainstorming, which allows for thoughtful and independent idea generation, is sometimes overlooked in group settings.

8. Hierarchy and Influence: Hierarchical structures within teams can influence brainstorming dynamics. Those in positions of authority may exert more influence, potentially steering the ideation process in a particular direction. This can restrict the free flow of ideas and hinder equal participation.

9. Cultural and Language Barriers: In global or diverse teams, language and cultural barriers may affect the effectiveness of group brainstorming. Not all team members may be equally proficient in the brainstorming language, potentially limiting their ability to contribute fully.

While acknowledging these limitations, it's important to recognize that group brainstorming remains a valuable tool when employed thoughtfully and complemented with other ideation approaches. An inclusive and psychologically safe environment is essential for encouraging diverse and uninhibited idea generation within the group setting. Additionally, a hybrid approach that combines group and individual brainstorming ensures that all team members have the opportunity to contribute their best ideas while mitigating the challenges posed by group dynamics.

"When you put a bunch of brainstormers in a room, it's like throwing spaghetti at the wall and hoping something sticks. Sometimes, it's just a messy room."

14 Execution Challenges

Another major challenge associated with Design Thinking is the struggle to implement and execute ideas. A variety of factors contribute to this struggle:

1. **Ideation-Execution Gap:** Design Thinking strongly encourages ideation and creative brainstorming, which often generate numerous innovative solutions. However, the transition from these ideas to actual implementation can be complex and challenging. Many promising concepts remain unexecuted, creating a gap between ideation and realization.

2. **Complex Problem-Solution Fit:** Some problems addressed through Design Thinking demand multifaceted solutions, which can be daunting and resource-intensive to implement. Aligning intricate solutions with complex issues can be an arduous process, impeding effective execution.

3. **Resource Limitations:** Execution requires resources such as funding, skilled personnel, and time. Limited resources can hinder the realization

of even the most groundbreaking ideas, making it a common barrier to implementation.

4. **Lack of Organizational Savvy:** Many designers may not possess in-depth knowledge of organizational culture, negotiation, and the skills required to influence decision-makers. Understanding the dynamics within the organization and identifying key stakeholders who can drive implementation is often overlooked.

5. **Organizational Resistance to Change:** The implementation of Design Thinking ideas can necessitate significant changes in existing systems, processes, and structures. Resistance to these changes can be formidable, creating reluctance to move forward with implementation.

6. **Inadequate Planning:** Effective execution demands comprehensive planning, including clearly defined objectives, timelines, and resource allocation. Rushing into execution without proper planning can lead to inefficiencies and unsuccessful outcomes.

7. **Lack of Alignment:** Ensuring alignment among team members and stakeholders regarding the goals and objectives of an idea is essential for successful execution. Misalignment can result in conflicting priorities and hinder the implementation process.

8. **People Management Skills:** A Design Thinking team needs people management skills to identify the right individuals for each task. In several cases, designers may hand over instructions for implementation without considering the challenges and variations in human behaviour in specific contexts.

9. **Measuring Success:** Organizations often struggle to define and assess Key Performance Indicators (KPIs) that indicate the success of Design Thinking initiatives, making it difficult to evaluate the impact of executed ideas.

10. **Sensory Presentations:** Design Thinking often relies heavily on visually and sensory representing ideas, which can bypass the analytical part of the brain and connect directly with emotions. This initial emotional response can create enthusiasm and excitement. However, this excitement can wane when practical challenges and limitations become apparent.

11. **Oversimplification:** Visual and sensory representations can oversimplify complex issues, leading to a narrow focus on certain solutions and neglecting important details. This limits the potential for successful implementation.

""Execution in design thinking: the part where you turn napkin sketches into business plans and hope it's more Picasso than preschool.""

The true value of Design Thinking lies not only in generating creative ideas but in realizing them as actionable and impactful outcomes.

In conclusion, Design Thinking is a valuable tool for solving certain types of problems, particularly user-centric ones. However, it may not be the best tool for driving broader business strategy and transformational change. Businesses should adopt a more holistic and integrated approach to innovation that considers multiple perspectives and frameworks. By doing so, they can stay ahead of the competition and drive growth in a rapidly changing market.

* * *

3

Limitations of the Diffusion of Innovation Model

The diffusion of innovation curve is a widely used model for understanding the adoption of new products, ideas, or technologies. It provides a framework for the stages of new product adoption, from the initial innovators and early adopters to the majority and laggards. While the curve has been useful in many contexts, it has limitations. In this chapter, we will explore some of the limitations of the diffusion of the innovation curve and why it is important to go beyond the curve to understand the complex factors that influence adoption.

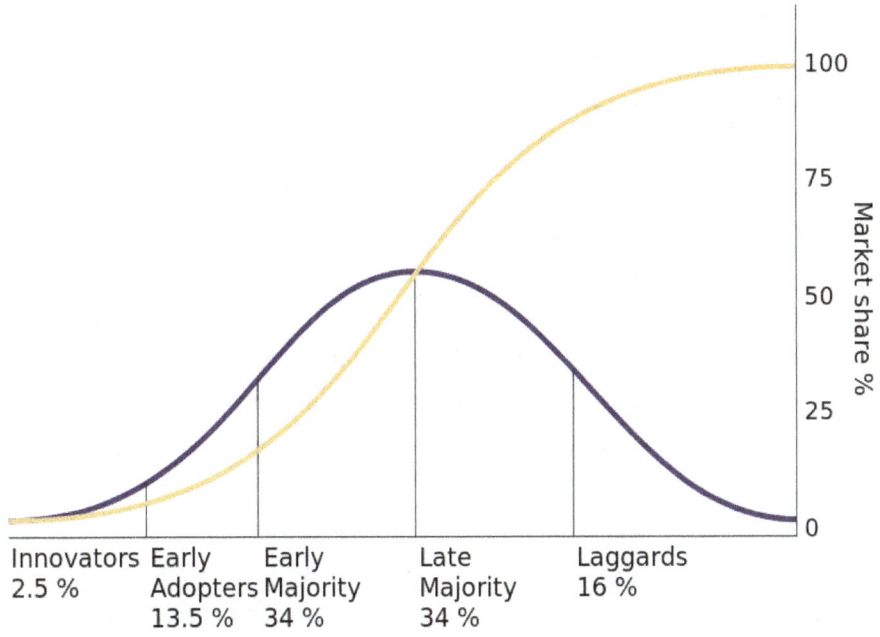

Image Source:: Wikipedia

Note: *While the Diffusion of Innovation model was originally developed to explain the adoption of innovations in general, it has since been applied to the adoption of new products specifically. As such, the terms "product adoption" and "innovation adoption" can be used interchangeably when discussing the adoption and diffusion of new products. Regardless of the terminology used, the factors influencing adoption and diffusion remain the same.*

Diffusion on Innovation Model

The diffusion of innovation refers to the process by which new products, ideas, or technologies are adopted and spread across a population. It is a process that can take place over a period of time, involving different stages and different types of adopters.

The diffusion of innovation model was first introduced by sociologist Everett Rogers in 1962. It is based on the idea that adoption occurs through communication and social influence. The model describes five stages of adoption: awareness(knowledge), interest(persuasion), evaluation(decision), trial(implementation), and adoption(confirmation).

According to the model, there are five types of adopters: innovators, early adopters, early majority, late majority, and laggards. Innovators are the first to adopt an innovation, and they are followed by early adopters, who are opinion leaders and often have a higher social status. The early majority adopts the innovation after it has become more widely known. They are followed by the late majority, who may adopt the innovation due to peer pressure or economic necessity. Laggards are the last to adopt the innovation, often due to traditional values and scepticism towards change.

The diffusion of innovation model also emphasizes the importance of communication and social influence in the adoption process. Innovations are often adopted through interpersonal communication, such as word-of-mouth, and mass media can also play a role in raising awareness and creating interest.

Benefits of Diffusion of Innovation Model

1. Targeted Marketing: The Diffusion of Innovation model is invaluable in identifying and targeting specific segments of the population based on their innovativeness. Innovators and early adopters, being the first to embrace new ideas, are ideal targets for the initial launch of innovative products or services. By understanding the characteristics and preferences of these groups, businesses can tailor their marketing efforts to resonate with these forward-thinking consumers. This can involve crafting messages that emphasize the uniqueness and trailblazing aspects of the offering, as these early adopters tend to be adventurous and open to trying new things.

As the innovation moves through the adoption curve, businesses can pivot their marketing strategies. The early majority requires different messaging and approaches. They are often influenced by feedback from early adopters and seek evidence of an innovation's widespread acceptance. Therefore, this stage might involve the use of testimonials, case studies, and clear indications of the innovation's benefits.

The late majority, who adopt innovations after the majority of the population, are typically more cautious and require reassurance. They might be swayed by messages that emphasize the innovation's proven track record, safety, and how it addresses common needs. Laggards may need the most persuasive communication to overcome their skepticism. The Diffusion of Innovation model guides businesses to adapt their marketing strategies to cater to these distinct stages, ensuring more effective engagement with each group.

2. Timing and Strategy: One of the core strengths of the Diffusion of Innovation model is its ability to provide insights into the timing and strategy for product or service launches. Understanding where an innovation stands within the adoption curve informs decisions about the right time to bring it to market and the most suitable strategies.

For innovators and early adopters, the emphasis may be on teasers and exclusive previews. These tactics generate excitement among early adopters, who appreciate being the first to experience something new. Providing sneak peeks, limited-access trials, or exclusive offers can be powerful in capturing their attention.

As the innovation progresses to the early and late majority, the focus shifts to providing evidence of its acceptance and benefits. Testimonials, reviews, and demonstrations play a vital role. These consumers look for social proof, and they need to see that others have already had positive experiences with the innovation.

3. Feedback and Iteration: The Diffusion of Innovation model offers a structured approach to gather feedback from different adopter groups, which is instrumental for iteration and improvement. By monitoring the diffusion process, businesses can understand how different segments of the population respond to the innovation and what factors influence their adoption decisions.

For innovators and early adopters, feedback can reveal how well the innovation aligns with their pioneering spirit. Their responses might highlight the need for even more cutting-edge features, functionalities, or unique selling points.

Feedback from the early and late majority can provide insights into what aspects of the innovation resonate most with them and what concerns they may have. This information guides iteration efforts to make the product or service more appealing and convincing.

4. Resource Allocation: The model also plays a crucial role in resource allocation. In the early stages of the adoption process, when dealing with innovators and early adopters, businesses can allocate limited resources for initial product development and marketing. This targeted approach ensures that the innovation reaches these early adopters without overstretching resources.

As the innovation gains acceptance and moves toward the early and late majority, businesses can invest more resources in scaling production, marketing, and distribution. This staged allocation of resources is both efficient and cost-effective.

5. Competitive Advantage: A clear understanding of the Diffusion of Innovation model equips companies with a competitive advantage. It enables them to stay ahead of competitors by identifying opportunities to introduce innovations more effectively and efficiently. This strategic advantage lies in the ability to anticipate how a new product or service will be adopted and how to engage various segments of the market at different stages of the adoption process.

By staying attuned to the preferences, needs, and adoption behaviours of various segments, businesses can outmanoeuvre competitors who lack this insight. As a result, they can maximize their market share, increase their reach, and establish a stronger foothold within their industry.

Diffusion of Innovation Model in Designing Products and Services

The Diffusion of Innovation model plays a significant role in designing innovative products or services tailored to different segments of adopters, such as innovators, early adopters, early majority, late majority, and laggards. Each segment has distinct preferences, expectations, and behaviours, which impact product design and development. Here's an in-depth exploration of how the model guides the design process for each segment:

1. **Innovators (2.5%):** Innovators are risk-takers who seek novelty and enjoy experimenting with new products or technologies. When designing for innovators, businesses can create products with advanced features, unique functionalities, and cutting-edge technology. These users are willing to invest time and effort in understanding complex interfaces and are open to unconventional solutions. The key is to emphasize innovation and creativity in product design.

2. **Early Adopters (13.5%):** Early adopters value being trendsetters and are motivated by the social recognition of being the first to try a new product. Designing for this segment involves focusing on user-friendly interfaces, superior quality, and seamless user experiences. Early adopters appreciate products that offer a balance between innovation and usability. User-centric design, elegant aesthetics, and a touch of sophistication are important considerations.

3. **Early Majority (34%):** The early majority consists of pragmatic users who adopt new products when they perceive clear advantages. They value ease of use, reliability, and convenience. Product design for the early majority should prioritize simplicity, efficiency, and affordability. Minimal cognitive load, intuitive interfaces, and straightforward setup processes are crucial. The design should emphasize mainstream appeal.

4. **Late Majority (34%):** Late majority adopters are typically skeptical of new products and only embrace them when they become well-established in the market. They seek products that require minimal effort to use. Designing for this segment should focus on reducing any barriers to adoption. Clarity,

simplicity, and proven functionality are key. Instruction manuals and customer support should be readily available.

5. Laggards (16%): Laggards are resistant to change and prefer traditional or well-established products. When designing for laggards, it's essential to ensure compatibility with existing systems or technologies. Simplicity, robustness, and familiarity are essential design principles. The product should require minimal adaptation or learning on the user's part.

The Diffusion of Innovation model acts as a guiding framework for designing innovative products or services that cater to the unique preferences and behaviours of different adopter segments. Understanding the distinct needs of each group ensures that products are well-received and have a higher chance of successful adoption.

Macintosh

The launch of Apple's Macintosh computer is a remarkable example of how the Diffusion of Innovation model can be applied in practice, even if the terminology used may not have been explicitly defined at the time. Apple's strategy for introducing the Macintosh demonstrates a clear understanding of the different adopter segments and how to leverage them for successful diffusion:

1. **Innovators (Early Graphic Artists and Designers):** Apple initially targeted innovators within the graphic design industry, recognizing that they were the individuals most likely to appreciate the Macintosh's cutting-edge Graphical User Interface (GUI) and its performance for design-related tasks. These early adopters were tech-savvy and willing to experiment with new technologies, making them the ideal starting point.

2. **Early Adopters (Graphic Designers' Clients, Marketing Professionals, Executives):** The early graphic artists and designers who embraced the Macintosh began using it to deliver presentations to marketing professionals and executives within their organizations. This shift marked the transition to the early adopter stage. The GUI and performance of the Macintosh were

particularly appealing to this group, leading to successful adoption.

3. Early Majority (Marketing and Sales Professionals): As marketing and sales professionals within these organizations recognized the advantages of the Macintosh, they began incorporating it into their work processes. The Macintosh's user-friendly GUI and responsiveness made it a practical choice for their tasks, which extended its reach further.

4. Late Majority (Outside Vendors, Publishers, Clients): The adoption of the Macintosh continued to spread as marketing and sales professionals used it to give presentations to external stakeholders, including vendors, publishers, and clients. The benefits of the Macintosh became increasingly evident to these late majority users, who were initially skeptical of the new technology.

5. Laggards (Remaining Market): While the majority of the market had adopted the Macintosh at this point, there may have still been some laggards who were hesitant to embrace the change. However, the positive feedback loop generated by the earlier adopter segments, along with the sense of social desirability surrounding Macintosh adoption, likely encouraged even some laggards to reconsider.

The Apple Macintosh's diffusion was accelerated by strategically targeting different adopter segments within a specific professional ecosystem. By recognizing the unique needs and preferences of each group and how they influenced one another, Apple created a ripple effect that contributed to the Macintosh's rapid and widespread adoption. This example showcases how a deep understanding of the Diffusion of Innovation model, even if not explicitly labeled as such, can be leveraged to successfully introduce new products to the market.

EDMS

The introduction of Documentum's Electronic Document Management System (EDMS) in 1993 provides an exemplary case of leveraging the Diffusion of Innovation model to drive the successful adoption of a transformative product. Documentum's strategy illustrates how understanding the needs and preferences of distinct adopter groups can lead to widespread diffusion:

1. Targeting Early Adopters (Regulatory Affairs in Pharmaceutical Companies): Documentum initially focused on a niche market — the regulatory affairs department in Fortune 500 pharmaceutical companies. These early adopters had a high user pain point, as they needed to manage and file an extensive volume of documents, ranging from 250,000 to 500,000. The EDMS was specifically tailored to address this significant pain point.

2. Creating Positive Feedback Loops: As regulatory affairs professionals in pharmaceutical companies began using the EDMS, they quickly recognized its benefits in streamlining their document management processes. This positive feedback loop played a crucial role in encouraging further adoption. The early adopters became advocates for the system, sharing their positive experiences.

3. Expanding to Related Departments: As the EDMS proved its value to the regulatory affairs department, its adoption naturally spread to other departments within the pharmaceutical companies. Departments involved in research and manufacturing, which regularly interacted with regulatory affairs and shared similar document management challenges, were next in line to embrace the solution.

4. Extending to External Stakeholders: The positive feedback and efficiency gains experienced within the pharmaceutical industry led to external vendors, contractors, and partners in the ecosystem adopting the EDMS. The system's reputation grew as a reliable and effective solution, enticing further stakeholders to participate in the diffusion.

5. Cross-Industry Diffusion: The diffusion process continued as the EDMS transcended the boundaries of the pharmaceutical sector. Industries facing analogous document management challenges, such as oil refineries and real estate, began adopting the EDMS. These late majority adopters recognized the benefits of the solution based on the positive experiences of early and early majority users in various fields.

Documentum's strategic approach, based on the Diffusion of Innovation model, effectively aligned with the unique pain points and needs of each adopter group. By addressing the specific challenges faced by regulatory affairs departments in pharmaceutical companies, Documentum paved the way for the widespread adoption and diffusion of its EDMS.

* * *

The Limitations of Diffusion of Innovation

What is the Need to Understand the Limitations?: Understanding the limitations of the Diffusion of Innovation Model is essential for several significant reasons. Firstly, recognizing these limitations provides a more comprehensive understanding of the model's applicability and scope. This depth of comprehension allows researchers, innovators, and businesses to make informed decisions about the model's effective use, preventing misguided reliance on it.

Moreover, these acknowledged limitations are essential for real-world applications. In practice, adoption scenarios often involve complex and multifaceted dynamics. Understanding where the model may fall short empowers practitioners to navigate these complexities more effectively. They can adapt their strategies to better align with the real-world adoption patterns, thereby enhancing the likelihood of success.

Identifying these limitations serves to encourage continuous improvement in innovation processes. Innovators can utilize these insights to refine their strategies, making innovations more successful and reducing the risk of failure. Addressing the model's shortcomings enables the development of more robust and effective approaches to innovation.

Furthermore, the limitations underscore the importance of considering cultural and contextual variations in adoption. In today's globalized world, innovations frequently cross cultural boundaries. Acknowledging these limitations reminds practitioners to account for cultural and contextual factors, ensuring that adoption strategies are culturally sensitive and contextually relevant.

Finally, discussing these limitations is critical to prevent overreliance on the model and promote a balanced approach to innovation adoption. While the model is a valuable tool, it is not universally applicable. Innovators and researchers should integrate multiple models and strategies to address the intricacies of adoption effectively.

In summary, understanding and acknowledging the limitations of the Diffusion of Innovation Model is vital for maximizing its utility, adapting to real-world scenarios, improving innovation processes, and promoting a well-rounded approach to innovation adoption.

Let's explore some of the limitations of the Diffusion of Innovation model.

01 The Assumption of Homogeneous Population

One of the limitations of the diffusion of innovation curve is the assumption of a homogeneous population. The curve assumes that all individuals in a population are the same, have equal access to information, and make decisions based on the same criteria. However, in reality, populations are heterogeneous, and individuals may have different preferences, values, and behaviours.

 *"Remember, assuming everyone's the same in innovation is as logical as expecting everyone at a buffet to fill their plates with the exact same food."*

EV Adoption: A notable example of the limitation of assuming a homogeneous population in the context of the Diffusion of Innovation Model can be seen in the adoption of electric vehicles (EVs). The diffusion of EVs represents a case where the assumption of a homogeneous population does not hold, and the diverse needs, preferences, and behaviours of individuals play a significant role.

a) Heterogeneous Preferences and Values: In the adoption of electric vehicles, it's evident that people have diverse preferences and values. While some individuals are enthusiastic about environmentally friendly transportation and are eager to adopt EVs due to their reduced carbon footprint, others prioritize factors like cost savings, convenience, or performance. This diversity in values and preferences creates distinct segments within the population.

- **Example**: Imagine a neighborhood in a large urban center where various people reside. In this neighborhood, there are environmentally conscious residents who are willing to pay a premium for an electric vehicle to reduce their carbon footprint. On the other hand, there are cost-conscious residents who prioritize the economic benefits of driving an EV, such as lower fuel and maintenance costs. These two groups within the same community have differing values and preferences, making it clear that the population is not homogeneous.

b) Differential Access to Information: The adoption of electric vehicles is also influenced by varying access to information. Some individuals have access to extensive information about EVs, including details about charging infrastructure, government incentives, and environmental benefits. In contrast, others may lack access to such information or may not be aware of the advantages of EV adoption.

- **Example**: Consider two co-workers in the same office who live in different neighbourhoods. One of them resides in an area where there are numerous charging stations for electric vehicles, and local government incentives are widely advertised. This individual has easy access to information about the benefits of EVs. The other co-worker lives in a neighbourhood with limited charging infrastructure and minimal information available. Their awareness and knowledge about EVs differ significantly, influencing their adoption decisions.

c) Diverse Adoption Criteria: Individuals often have different criteria for making adoption decisions. Some may prioritize environmental impact, while others focus on financial savings, range, or the availability of charging infrastructure. This diversity in adoption criteria further underscores the heterogeneity of the population.

- **Example**: In a family setting, one member might be primarily concerned about the environmental benefits of electric vehicles and is willing to accept a shorter range in exchange for a reduced carbon footprint. Another family member might be more concerned about practicality and insists on an EV with a longer range and the availability of charging options, even if it comes at a higher cost. These differing criteria within the same family demonstrate that the population is far from homogeneous.

In this context, the assumption of a homogeneous population in the Diffusion of Innovation Model doesn't align with the reality of EV adoption. To effectively promote the diffusion of EVs, it's essential to acknowledge and address the diverse preferences, values, access to information, and criteria within the population. This recognition leads to tailored strategies that resonate with different segments of the population, helping to accelerate the adoption of electric vehicles.

02 The Linear Process Assumption

Another limitation of the diffusion of the innovation curve is the assumption of a linear adoption process. The curve assumes that the adoption process follows a linear path, from early adopters to laggards, and that the adoption rate is constant over time. However, in reality, the adoption process rarely follows a straightforward, linear trajectory. Instead, it can involve dynamic and complex interactions among different groups of adopters, each influencing the other. These interactions can lead to rapid shifts in adoption rates and can make the process highly non-linear.

1. **Early Adopters Influencing Early Majority**: Early adopters, who are known for their enthusiasm and willingness to take risks, may influence the early majority more quickly than the model suggests. Their positive experiences, endorsements, and early adoption behaviors can lead to a more rapid diffusion of an innovation to the early majority.

2. **Early Majority Influencing Late Majority**: The early majority, often considered a bridge between early adopters and the late majority, can play a pivotal role in accelerating adoption. Their adoption decisions can influence the more skeptical late majority by providing real-world examples of successful implementation.

3. **Late Majority Influencing Early Adopters**: Sometimes, the late majority's adoption of an innovation can circle back to influence early adopters. This can happen when early adopters observe that the innovation is gaining widespread acceptance and decide to re-evaluate their choices.

Several factors contribute to the non-linear nature of the adoption process:

- **Communication and Social Networks**: Communication channels and social networks play a significant role in shaping the non-linear adoption process. The rapid spread of information through social media and online communities can lead to sudden surges in adoption.
- **External Events**: External events, such as a major crisis or technological breakthrough, can disrupt the linear path. For example, the COVID-19 pandemic accelerated the adoption of remote work technologies that were once in the domain of early adopters.
- **Regulatory Changes**: Changes in regulations or policies can also cause non-linear adoption. When new regulations incentivize or mandate the adoption of certain technologies or practices, the rate of adoption can experience rapid shifts.
- **Market Forces**: Economic factors and market dynamics can lead to non-linear adoption. The emergence of disruptive innovations or the entry of new competitors can cause abrupt changes in adoption patterns.
- **Feedback Loop:** The adoption process can be influenced by feedback

loops, where early adopters influence the adoption behaviour of the early majority, which then influences the late majority, creating a positive reinforcement effect. This leads to an accelerated and non-linear adoption pattern.

- **Bifurcation Effect:** The adoption process can also be influenced by discontinuities or disruptions, such as the emergence of a more disruptive innovation. In such cases, individuals may abandon the current innovation and switch to the new one, creating a bifurcation effect where the adoption splits into two paths.

In summary, recognizing the limitation of assuming a linear adoption process in the Diffusion of Innovation Model is vital for crafting effective strategies that can adapt to the complex, real-world patterns of innovation diffusion. Understanding the dynamic interactions among adopter groups and the influence of external factors is essential for businesses and innovators to navigate the non-linear nature of innovation adoption successfully.

"If innovation adoption were linear, we'd all be wearing bell-bottoms and listening to disco, waiting for the next 'big' thing."

The limitation of assuming a linear adoption process in the Diffusion of Innovation Model suggests that strategies for promoting adoption should be flexible and adaptable. The marketing and communication efforts should be prepared for sudden shifts in adoption rates and be responsive to the complex, non-linear nature of the process.

Examples of Non-linear Innovations:

Several real-world innovations have experienced non-linear adoption patterns, deviating from the linear path presumed by the Diffusion of Innovation Model. Here are a few examples:

Smartphones:

- **Linear Assumption**: The Diffusion of Innovation Model would suggest a steady increase in smartphone adoption over time.
- **Non-Linear Adoption**: The adoption of smartphones witnessed an explosive and non-linear growth due to several factors, including rapid technological advancements, the introduction of revolutionary features, and the creation of an "Apple effect" that spurred imitation and competition among manufacturers. The adoption accelerated beyond early adopters and reached the early majority faster than predicted.

Social Media: The adoption of social media platforms, like Facebook and Instagram, experienced non-linear growth due to network effects. As more people joined, the platforms became more attractive to others, creating a self-reinforcing cycle. The exponential growth exceeded the expectations of linear models.

Electric Vehicles (EVs): Linear adoption models might anticipate a slow and steady increase in the adoption of electric vehicles. However, the adoption of electric vehicles saw non-linear growth due to advancements in battery technology, government incentives, and a heightened focus on sustainability. As charging infrastructure expanded and driving range increased, the adoption rate accelerated, particularly among the early majority.

Online Streaming Services: The adoption of online streaming services, like Netflix and Amazon Prime Video, experienced non-linear growth. The ease of access, original content production, and word-of-mouth recommendations created rapid adoption, moving beyond early adopters to reach a global audience.

These examples illustrate that many innovations experience non-linear adoption patterns due to a variety of factors, including technology advancements, network effects, regulatory changes, and shifts in consumer behaviour. Such non-linear adoption can challenge the assumptions of a linear adoption model like the Diffusion of Innovation Model.

03 Cultural and Contextual Variations

The Diffusion of Innovation Model may not be universally applicable across different cultures. Cultural and contextual variations can influence the adoption process and the model's applicability might differ from one culture to another:

1. **Cultural Values and Norms**: Different cultures have unique values and norms that shape consumer behaviour. What is considered innovative, acceptable, or desirable can vary widely between cultures. For example, individualistic cultures may prioritise personal choice and innovation, while collectivist cultures may value tradition and conformity.
2. **Communication Styles**: Communication patterns also differ across cultures. Some cultures may rely on word-of-mouth and personal networks for information and recommendations, while others may be more influenced by formal advertising and expert endorsements.
3. **Trust and Skepticism**: The level of trust in institutions, brands, and other consumers can vary between cultures. High levels of trust can expedite the adoption process, while skepticism can slow it down.
4. **Economic Factors**: Economic conditions and income disparities vary across cultures. Affordability and perceived value play a significant role in the adoption of new products. A product considered affordable in one culture might be a luxury in another.
5. **Legal and Regulatory Environment**: Legal and regulatory frameworks differ worldwide. Certain innovations may face more significant barriers in some countries due to regulatory restrictions or intellectual property issues.
6. **Local Competition**: The competitive landscape can also influence adoption. Local alternatives and established players may deter the

adoption of new innovations, particularly if they are deeply entrenched in a market.

7. **Social Structures**: Social hierarchies, family structures, and community dynamics vary across cultures. These structures can impact how information is disseminated, how decisions are made, and who influences the adoption process.

8. **Socioeconomic Factors**: Socioeconomic disparities are pronounced globally. What might be accessible to an affluent segment of the population in one culture could be beyond the reach of the majority in another.

9. **Language and Communication Barriers**: Language barriers can hinder the spread of innovations. The language of communication and marketing materials must be accessible to the target audience.

10. **Cultural Perceptions of Risk**: Some cultures may be more risk-averse, while others may embrace novelty. The perception of risk can significantly influence the willingness to adopt innovations.

11. **Consumer Behavior Patterns**: How consumers research, evaluate, and make purchasing decisions can vary. Some cultures may engage in extensive research, while others rely on emotional or impulsive decision-making.

Given these variations, the adoption of innovations can follow different trajectories in diverse cultural contexts. The Diffusion of Innovation Model may need to be adapted or supplemented with cultural insights and contextual understanding when applied to different regions or communities. Acknowledging these cultural and contextual variations is essential for successful innovation adoption in a globalized world.

"Trying to apply the same innovation model in every culture is like serving ice cream at the North Pole - it might not melt, but it won't make sense either."

Here are some examples of variations in adoption behaviour due to cultural factors:

1. **Food and Dietary Preferences**: Cultural factors play a significant role in food adoption behavior. For example, while sushi is a widely adopted and beloved dish in Japan, it may be met with resistance or hesitation in cultures where raw fish consumption is less common.

2. **Traditional Clothing**: The adoption of traditional clothing is highly influenced by cultural factors. In cultures where traditional attire holds deep significance, such as the Indian saree or the Japanese kimono, adoption is driven by cultural preservation and identity.

3. **Language Learning Apps**: In some cultures, there is a strong emphasis on learning and preserving the native language. Adoption of language learning apps may be higher in regions where language and culture are closely intertwined.

4. **Religious Practices**: Cultural variations in religious practices lead to differences in adoption. For example, the use of meditation and prayer apps may be more prevalent in cultures where meditation and prayer are integral to daily life.

5. **Marriage Customs**: Cultural variations in marriage customs lead to differences in the adoption of wedding-related products and services. Wedding traditions, attire, and ceremonies vary widely among cultures, impacting adoption choices.

6. **Entertainment Preferences**: Cultural preferences for entertainment can greatly affect adoption behavior. While traditional theater performances may have a strong following in some cultures, others may prefer modern cinema or digital streaming.

7. **Health and Wellness Practices**: The adoption of health and wellness practices can be shaped by cultural beliefs. For instance, practices like yoga and Ayurveda are more likely to be adopted in cultures where they have historical and cultural roots.

8. **Consumer Electronics**: Cultural factors impact the adoption of consumer electronics. For example, the design and features of smartphones

or other devices may need to align with cultural preferences and values.

9. **Educational Methods**: Cultural attitudes toward education vary. Adoption of educational methods, whether traditional or innovative, is influenced by cultural values related to knowledge and learning.

10. **Automobile Preferences**: Different cultures have distinct preferences for automobiles. In some cultures, smaller and more fuel-efficient vehicles may be favored, while in others, larger and more luxurious cars may be preferred.

11. **Societal Roles and Gender Norms**: Cultural norms regarding gender roles and societal expectations can influence adoption behavior. For example, adoption of gender-specific products or services may be shaped by cultural attitudes toward gender equality.

12. **Greeting Practices**: The adoption of greeting practices and communication tools may vary. Some cultures have specific greetings and etiquettes, which may affect the adoption of messaging apps or video conferencing platforms.

These examples demonstrate how deeply cultural factors impact the adoption of products, services, and practices. Understanding these cultural nuances is essential for businesses and innovators seeking to introduce their offerings in diverse global markets. Tailoring products and marketing strategies to align with cultural preferences and values can greatly enhance adoption rates.

04 Assumption of Rational Decision Making

The Diffusion of Innovation model assumes that individuals make rational decisions based on a careful evaluation of information and a weighing of the innovation's advantages. However, in reality, human decision-making is often influenced by emotional and psychological factors, which can pose a significant limitation to the model.

1. **Emotional Decision-Making:** Human beings are not purely rational creatures; emotions play a significant role in decision-making. Emotions

like fear, excitement, nostalgia, and desire can strongly influence whether an individual chooses to adopt an innovation.

In recent years, there has been a resurgence in the popularity of vintage-style vinyl records, despite the prevalence of digital music streaming and high-quality audio formats. This adoption of a seemingly outdated technology can be attributed to emotional decision-making.

While digital music offers convenience and a vast library of songs, vinyl records evoke nostalgia and a sense of authenticity. Many music enthusiasts, particularly those from older generations, find the tactile and analog nature of vinyl records emotionally appealing. The act of placing the needle on a record, hearing the subtle crackles, and viewing the large album artwork triggers emotions associated with cherished memories and a connection to the music.

In this case, emotional factors, such as nostalgia and a desire for a tangible and immersive music experience, influence the adoption of vinyl records, even among individuals who have access to more technologically advanced music formats. This emotional decision-making deviates from the rational progression outlined in the Diffusion of Innovation model, where adoption is primarily driven by perceived advantages and logical considerations.

2. Cognitive Biases: People are subject to various cognitive biases, such as confirmation bias (preferring information that confirms their existing beliefs), anchoring (relying too heavily on the first piece of information encountered), and loss aversion (being more averse to loss than enticed by gain). These biases can lead to decisions that don't align with a rational evaluation of an innovation's merits.

3. Social Influence: The opinions and behaviours of others can have a powerful impact on an individual's decisions. People often adopt innovations because they see others around them doing so, not necessarily because they've rationally analyzed the innovation's benefits. This is known as social proof or herd behavior.

4. Perceived Risk: Emotions like fear can lead to a perception of risk, which can inhibit innovation adoption. People may be afraid of the potential downsides, even if they rationally understand the potential benefits.

5. Psychological Barriers: Individuals may have psychological barriers to adopting innovations, such as a resistance to change or a preference for the familiar. These barriers are deeply rooted in emotions and can override rational assessment.

6. Emotional Appeal: Marketing and communication strategies often use emotional appeal to trigger adoption. For example, advertisements may aim to evoke feelings of happiness, nostalgia, or belonging, which can lead to emotional decision-making.

7. Delayed Gratification: The model assumes that individuals make decisions based on a rational evaluation of long-term benefits. However, many people are more inclined to choose immediate gratification over long-term gain due to the emotional rewards of instant satisfaction.

8. The Role of Stories and Narratives: People often make decisions based on the narratives or stories surrounding an innovation. The emotional resonance of a compelling story can outweigh a rational assessment of an innovation's features.

9. Impulse Buying: Impulse purchases and adoption can be driven by emotional impulses, such as a sudden desire for a product triggered by an emotional response.

Considering the emotional and psychological aspects of decision-making is vital for a more nuanced understanding of how innovations are adopted. This limitation of the model reminds us that innovation adoption is not solely a rational process but one deeply intertwined with human emotions and psychological factors. To effectively promote adoption, innovators and businesses must be attuned to the emotional drivers that influence individual choices.

"The innovation model's faith in rational decision-making is as optimistic as expecting a toddler to understand complex algebra - cute, but not going to happen."

A Few Examples—

1. **Apple's Marketing Success:** Apple has been exceptionally skilled at using emotional appeal to drive product adoption. Their advertisements often evoke feelings of creativity, innovation, and a sense of belonging to a forward-thinking community. The emotional connection people have with Apple products goes beyond their rational features, leading to strong adoption rates.

2. **Fast Food Advertising:** Fast-food chains like McDonald's and Burger King employ tactics that trigger emotional desires for their products. They use vibrant visuals, humor, and enticing narratives to create an emotional connection with their offerings. This emotional appeal often outweighs rational concerns about health and nutrition.

3. **Luxury Brands:** High-end luxury brands, such as Louis Vuitton and Rolex, primarily rely on emotional appeals. People purchase these products not just for their quality but because they symbolize prestige, success, and exclusivity. The emotional satisfaction of owning a luxury item can far surpass a rational analysis of its practicality.

4. **FOMO and Social Media:** The Fear of Missing Out (FOMO) is an emotional driver often leveraged by social media platforms. People adopt new apps, features, or trends because they don't want to feel left out of social conversations and experiences. This is a classic example of how emotional concerns can outweigh rational decision-making.

5. **Cult Brands:** Companies like Harley-Davidson and Red Bull have cultivated strong emotional connections with their customers. Harley-Davidson, for instance, is not just about motorcycles; it's about freedom, rebellion, and a sense of identity. These emotional elements are central to their products' appeal.

6. **Impulse Buying:** Impulse buying is driven by a sudden emotional desire. For example, a shopper may see a beautifully presented dessert in a bakery, and the emotional craving for a sweet treat outweighs any rational dietary considerations.

7. **Charitable Donations:** People often make donations to charities and causes due to emotional triggers. Heart-wrenching stories or images can evoke sympathy and a desire to help, prompting a donation despite

any rational assessment of the organization's effectiveness.

8. **In-Game Purchases:** In the world of gaming, players often make in-game purchases driven by emotional impulses like competitiveness, the desire to stand out, or the fear of missing out on exclusive items.

These examples highlight that emotional factors can strongly influence product adoption, often overriding rational evaluations of a product's features or benefits. Marketers and innovators recognize this and use emotional triggers strategically to drive adoption and sales. It's a reminder that human decision-making is a complex interplay of emotions and rationality, and both aspects must be considered in product adoption strategies.

05 Limited Predictive Accuracy

The Diffusion of Innovation model has limitations when it comes to accurately predicting adoption rates. These limitations stem from several factors:

1. **Complex Real-World Variables:** The model assumes a simplified environment where innovation is introduced to a homogenous population through a linear process. In reality, the adoption landscape is complex and influenced by various unpredictable variables such as economic conditions, cultural shifts, external events, and competing innovations. These real-world complexities make it challenging to predict adoption rates with precision.

2. **Changing Technology Landscape:** In today's rapidly evolving technological landscape, innovations can spread at unpredictable rates. The emergence of disruptive technologies, changes in consumer preferences, and rapid shifts in market dynamics can lead to adoption rates that deviate from the model's predictions.

3. **Black Swan Events:** The model does not account for outlier events, often referred to as "black swans," which have a substantial impact on adoption rates. These unforeseen events, such as pandemics, wars, or

economic crises, can significantly accelerate or decelerate the adoption of innovations, making predictions unreliable.

4. **Non-Linear Adoption:** As discussed earlier, the assumption of a linear adoption process oversimplifies the complex interactions among different adopter groups. These interactions can lead to non-linear adoption patterns, making it challenging to predict when an innovation will reach critical mass or achieve widespread adoption.

5. **Individual Variability:** The model does not consider the variations in individual adoption behaviour. While it categorizes adopters into broad groups, the actual behaviour of individuals within these groups can vary widely. Some early adopters may adopt immediately, while others may take their time, creating unpredictability in the adoption curve.

6. **Limited Data Precision:** Predicting adoption rates requires accurate data, and gathering precise data on innovation adoption can be challenging. Data collection and analysis often rely on surveys, which may not capture the full complexity of adoption behaviours, especially in today's digital age.

7. **Shortcomings in Data Collection:** Data collection challenges, including response bias and the time lag between data collection and reporting, can impact predictive accuracy. These limitations can lead to discrepancies between predicted and actual adoption rates.

8. **Model Assumptions:** The model's assumptions about the relative advantage, compatibility, complexity, trialability, and observability of an innovation may not always hold true. If an innovation's actual attributes deviate from these assumptions, predictions can be inaccurate.

9. **Behavioral Shifts:** The model does not account for significant shifts in human behavior that can alter adoption patterns. For example, the widespread adoption of smartphones fundamentally changed how people access information and interact with technology, challenging existing adoption predictions.

These limitations remind us that while the Diffusion of Innovation model provides a valuable framework for understanding adoption, its predictive accuracy is constrained by the complexity and unpredictability of real-world adoption scenarios. Innovators and businesses should use the model as a guide but be prepared to adapt to unforeseen variables and shifts in the adoption landscape.

"The model's prediction game is as precise as throwing darts blindfolded - you might hit the target, but chances are you'll miss."

A Few Examples—

Here are a few examples where innovations did not follow the model's anticipated adoption patterns:

1. **Instant Messaging Apps:** The adoption of instant messaging apps like WhatsApp and Facebook Messenger did not conform to traditional diffusion patterns. While these apps quickly gained popularity, they didn't necessarily start with innovators or early adopters. Instead, they became widely adopted across various age groups and demographics, challenging the model's expectations.

2. **Mobile Phones in Developing Countries:** The rapid adoption of mobile phones in developing countries, particularly in sub-Saharan Africa, was not initially expected. These regions experienced a leapfrog effect, where mobile phone adoption skipped landlines and spread quickly. The model's linear progression did not account for this non-linear adoption pattern.

3. **Electric Vehicles (EVs):** The diffusion of electric vehicles defies the model's predictions. EV adoption is influenced by various factors, including government incentives, environmental concerns, and advancements in battery technology. The model does not fully capture the dynamic nature of these influences, leading to unpredictable adoption rates.

4. **Social Media Platforms:** The rise of social media platforms, such as

Facebook and Twitter, challenged traditional diffusion patterns. These platforms gained mass adoption relatively quickly and appealed to a broad range of users. The model's predictions did not align with the widespread and diverse adoption of these platforms.

5. **Smart Home Devices:** Innovations in smart home technology, like smart speakers and thermostats, saw varied adoption patterns. While early adopters embraced these devices, the adoption curve was not as steep as the model might suggest. The diffusion of these innovations was influenced by factors like privacy concerns and compatibility issues, which the model does not explicitly account for.

6. **Telehealth Services:** The COVID-19 pandemic accelerated the adoption of telehealth services, with many individuals and healthcare providers adopting these technologies. The model did not anticipate this rapid shift and the influence of external events on adoption behavior.

7. **Cryptocurrencies:** The diffusion of cryptocurrencies like Bitcoin has been marked by unpredictability. While some individuals quickly adopted cryptocurrencies as innovators or early adopters, the broader public's acceptance followed a less conventional trajectory, with fluctuations driven by market dynamics and regulatory developments.

8. **E-commerce:** The model could not foresee the rapid growth of e-commerce, driven by factors like convenience, access to a broader range of products, and the rise of online marketplaces. The adoption of online shopping did not align with the model's traditional diffusion curve.

These cases illustrate how the Diffusion of Innovation model's predictions can fall short in capturing the intricate and often non-linear nature of adoption behaviors. Real-world innovations are subject to diverse influences, making it challenging to anticipate their adoption trajectories accurately.

06 The Impact of Marketing and Advertising

The role of marketing and advertising in shaping product adoption rates can be substantial, and their influence often transcends the traditional Diffusion of Innovation Model.

> *"An advertisement walks into a bar. The Innovators order a drink right away, the Early Adopters want to know what's on the specials, the Early Majority are convinced to try something new, the Late Majority consider it after two more rounds, and the Laggards... well, they're still reading the menu."*

Here's how marketing and advertising can drastically change product adoption rates and why they may not align with the model:

a) Accelerated Awareness and Interest: Effective marketing and advertising campaigns can rapidly increase awareness of a new product, creating a buzz around it. By framing the product as revolutionary or a must-have, marketers can generate heightened interest and curiosity, even among those who might not typically be early adopters.

While the Diffusion of Innovation Model suggests a gradual progression from early adopters to the early and late majority, marketing can potentially leapfrog this process. A compelling marketing campaign can pull in early and late majority consumers who are enticed by the hype, thus altering the predicted diffusion curve.

Example: Tesla's marketing was exceptionally effective in raising awareness. They used sleek, high-end branding, charismatic CEO Elon Musk, and a focus on innovation. This attracted not only early adopters but also a segment of the early and late majority who were intrigued by the idea of owning a technologically advanced, environmentally friendly vehicle.

In the traditional diffusion model, electric cars were expected to follow a slow progression from early adopters to the early and late majority over an extended period. However, Tesla's disruptive marketing campaigns and the allure of their cutting-edge electric cars altered this predicted curve. Many early and late majority consumers were enticed by the hype, causing an expedited adoption rate.

b) Influence on Early Majority: Marketing and advertising can focus on addressing the concerns and needs of the early majority. By providing evidence of the product's practicality, reliability, and widespread acceptance, these strategies can persuade the early majority to adopt the innovation sooner than anticipated by the model.

An example that illustrates the influence of marketing on the early majority can be seen in the adoption of smartphones. When smartphones were first introduced, they were considered a niche product mainly used by early adopters who were tech-savvy and eager to try new innovations.

However, Apple's marketing and advertising for the iPhone played a significant role in bridging the gap between early adopters and the early majority. Apple focused on highlighting the practicality, ease of use, and real-world applications of the iPhone. Their "There's an app for that" campaign, for instance, showcased how the device could address various everyday needs.

This targeted messaging not only accelerated the adoption of the iPhone but also influenced the early majority to embrace the technology earlier than expected by the traditional diffusion model. Instead of waiting for early adopters' reviews, many consumers were persuaded by Apple's marketing messages that directly addressed their practical concerns and needs.

c) Network Effects: Marketing and advertising often leverage social proof through testimonials, reviews, and endorsements. This can trigger a bandwagon effect, where potential adopters perceive the product as more desirable due to its popularity among others.

The Diffusion of Innovation Model doesn't account for the sudden surges in adoption driven by the bandwagon effect. Rather than a gradual curve, adoption can sometimes experience rapid spikes as marketing efforts capitalize on social proof.

A notable example of marketing leveraging social proof and causing rapid adoption is the case of the social media platform Facebook. When Facebook initially launched in 2004, it started as a platform exclusively for Harvard University students. As it expanded to other universities and eventually to the general public, it utilized a strategy of requiring a university email address to join. This exclusivity strategy created a sense of social proof – if you were part of a university network, you were part of an exclusive community.

As Facebook continued to grow, it launched aggressive marketing campaigns that emphasized the idea of "everyone" being on Facebook. Their slogan, "Facebook is a social utility that connects you with the people around you," reinforced the idea of widespread adoption. Additionally, they introduced the concept of the "News Feed," which highlighted user activity and interactions, creating a sense of social validation and proof.

These marketing strategies led to rapid adoption beyond the early adopter phase, with people from various demographics joining the platform in large numbers. Facebook's marketing efforts successfully harnessed the bandwagon effect by promoting social proof, and this kind of accelerated adoption isn't fully accounted for in the traditional Diffusion of Innovation model.

d) Cultural Adaptation: Marketers can tailor their messaging to resonate with different cultural or regional audiences, making the product more appealing to a diverse range of potential adopters.

When marketing efforts are adapted to diverse cultural backgrounds, adoption rates might not conform to a uniform diffusion curve. Instead, the adoption process can become more varied and influenced by cultural factors.

e) Negative Impacts: If marketing and advertising campaigns overpromise and underdeliver, they can lead to disillusionment among early adopters and the early majority. This disillusionment may disrupt the smooth progression described in the model.

In some cases, marketing claims may attract regulatory scrutiny or legal actions. These challenges may alter adoption rates, particularly if the marketing practices are considered unethical or misleading.

One example of marketing claims attracting regulatory scrutiny and impacting adoption rates is the case of Theranos, a health technology company. Theranos claimed to have revolutionized blood testing by offering a wide range of tests with just a few drops of blood. Through intense marketing and advertising efforts, the company garnered significant attention and investment.

However, as regulatory agencies and independent investigations delved into the technology and claims, it became clear that Theranos had overstated its capabilities. The company faced legal actions, and its founder, Elizabeth Holmes, was charged with massive fraud.

The regulatory constraints and legal actions against Theranos disrupted its adoption trajectory significantly. The overhyped marketing claims led to a loss of credibility and trust, ultimately affecting the adoption rates of the technology. This case illustrates how marketing can influence adoption both positively and negatively, and how regulatory constraints can intervene when marketing practices are deemed misleading or unethical.

f) Continuous Engagement: Marketing and advertising continue after adoption to reinforce the value of the product. This can help maintain high adoption rates even among the late majority and laggards.

In the traditional model, the late majority and laggards are portrayed as resistant to change. However, sustained marketing efforts can influence these segments, ensuring that they adopt the product over time.

An example of continuous post-adoption marketing influencing the late majority and laggards is the widespread adoption of smartphones. When smartphones were initially introduced, early adopters and the early majority embraced the new technology due to its novel features and capabilities.

However, the late majority and laggards, often more resistant to change, were initially hesitant to adopt smartphones. Continuous marketing efforts by smartphone manufacturers and service providers highlighted the practical benefits, such as easy communication, access to information, and various apps that could simplify daily tasks.

Over time, sustained marketing campaigns, promotions, and educational content appealed to the late majority and laggards. These segments gradually recognized the value of smartphones in their daily lives, leading to increased adoption rates among these groups. As a result, the adoption curve for smartphones deviated from the traditional model, with late majority and laggards adopting the technology later than predicted by the model. This example demonstrates how continuous post-adoption marketing can influence even the most resistant segments of the population.

In summary, marketing and advertising possess the unique capability to bend and mold the trajectory of product adoption rates. While the Diffusion of Innovation Model provides a valuable framework for understanding the general path of adoption, marketing and advertising can be powerful forces that disrupt, accelerate, or reshape the predicted adoption curve. Their potential to alter adoption rates, both positively and negatively, highlights the need for innovators and businesses to recognize the dynamic interplay between marketing strategies and the diffusion of innovations.

07 The Role of Social Influence

Social influence is a fundamental driver in the adoption and diffusion of innovations. It refers to the profound impact that individuals or groups have on an individual's attitudes, beliefs, and behaviours. This influence often operates outside the boundaries of traditional customer segments outlined in the diffusion of innovation model, allowing for a more dynamic and unpredictable adoption landscape.

a) Opinion Leaders: Individuals tend to be more inclined to adopt an innovation if they perceive it as popular within their social network or observe others in that network readily embracing it. This inherent social influence effect can be harnessed strategically to boost adoption by targeting specific individuals who play pivotal roles in their communities. Among these influencers, opinion leaders stand out as key figures who can significantly affect the attitudes and behaviors of those in their social circles.

Opinion leaders are individuals who possess the charisma and credibility to sway the opinions and choices of others within their social networks. They often exhibit a higher willingness to embrace innovations and are prone to adopting them early on. Innovators recognize opinion leaders as a critical focus for accelerating the diffusion of their innovations. By reaching out to these opinion leaders and cultivating a sense of social desirability around the innovation, they can amplify the likelihood of widespread adoption.

India serves as an intriguing example of the far-reaching impact of social influence, where religious leaders hold a prominent role in shaping the attitudes and behaviours of their followers across diverse customer segments. These revered figures possess the capacity to influence product adoption, effectively blurring the distinctions between conventional customer segments like early adopters, early majority, and late majority.

The endorsements and recommendations made by religious leaders within the Indian context carry substantial weight, inspiring trust and confidence among their followers. This influence is not confined to a specific customer segment, as religious leaders often draw followers from various socioeconomic backgrounds, educational levels, and age groups. Consequently, their guidance and support can influence adoption across different segments, creating a significant departure from the traditional diffusion of innovation model's linear progression.

This illustration of social influence's power in India emphasizes its ability to transcend the conventional boundaries of adoption and diffusion. It highlights the need for innovators to be attentive to the influence wielded by opinion leaders and other social influencers, regardless of their followers' demographic characteristics. By doing so, innovators can break free from the constraints of the traditional model, achieve more widespread adoption, and navigate the intricate dynamics of social influence in innovation diffusion.

b) Peer Pressure and Conformity: Social influence can exert significant pressure on individuals, compelling them to align their choices with those of their peers. When a product or innovation becomes popular within a specific social group, the desire to belong and gain acceptance drives rapid adoption.

This effect can lead to even those who aren't typically early adopters joining the bandwagon.

The intense peer pressure can induce a non-linear and accelerated adoption curve, causing a product to swiftly transition from innovators to a wide-scale adoption by the early and late majority due to the powerful influence of social networks.

Viral trends and challenges on social media platforms like TikTok exemplify this phenomenon. Such trends can showcase new products or innovations to a specific demographic, prompting rapid adoption. For instance, a viral challenge featuring a novel skateboard or sporting gear can trigger a surge in adoption among young users who wish to participate in the trend.

c) Celebrity Endorsements and Influencers: The endorsements of celebrities and social media influencers can wield profound influence on product adoption. Individuals often trust and emulate these prominent figures, leading to substantial increases in adoption rates when they endorse a product or innovation.

While the diffusion of innovation model implies a linear progression from early adopters to laggards, celebrity endorsements and influencer marketing can generate abrupt spikes in adoption. The broad and diverse audience reached through these endorsements often spans beyond traditional adopter categories.

Consider the endorsement of a skincare product by a well-known celebrity. Their testimonial can resonate with a broad audience, including individuals who aren't typically early adopters. This resonance can lead to a rapid upsurge in adoption rates, diverging from the model's predicted linear progression.

d) Social Network Effects: Social networks can facilitate the swift dissemination of information and trends. When a product or innovation gains traction within a particular social network, it can swiftly proliferate through that network, inducing a wave of adoption.

Within specific social networks, adoption rates can be accelerated, generating pockets of rapid adoption that don't conform to the linear model. Adoption within these networks can outpace the general population's adoption.

Professional networks offer an excellent example. The adoption of a new software tool or platform can rapidly spread within such networks. When a few influential members of the network adopt the innovation, their colleagues and connections may follow suit. This phenomenon can result in the innovation being adopted more rapidly within that specific network than the model predicts.

e) Online Communities and Reviews: Online communities and user reviews can significantly impact potential adopters' decisions. Positive reviews and shared experiences within these communities can lead to higher adoption rates, as individuals trust the recommendations of their peers.

Online forums dedicated to specific hobbies, such as photography, can sway the adoption of new camera equipment. When community members share their positive experiences with a particular camera brand or model, others within the community may be more inclined to adopt the same equipment. This peer influence can lead to faster adoption among community members than the model would predict.

In summary, social influence stands as a significant force in reshaping product adoption rates. Whether through peer pressure, celebrity endorsements, social networks, or online communities, social influence often leads to non-linear and accelerated adoption, defying the traditional diffusion of innovation model's predictions. Recognizing and harnessing the power of social influence is crucial for businesses and innovators aiming to effectively promote their products and innovations.

08 The Timing Factor

The Diffusion of Innovation model, while valuable in understanding how innovations spread, does not explicitly account for the role of timing.

Innovators must carefully consider the timing of their innovation's introduction to ensure that it aligns with market conditions and customer needs. If innovation is introduced too early, there may not be sufficient market demand or infrastructure to support its adoption. Conversely, if an innovation is introduced too late, competitors may have already captured the market, making it difficult for the innovation to gain traction.

Timing can also play a role in the diffusion of an innovation. Innovations introduced during rapid change or disruption, such as economic or technological upheaval, may be more readily adopted as individuals and organizations seek new solutions to navigate these changes.

When an innovation enters the market at precisely the right moment, it has the potential to disrupt the traditional adoption curve proposed by the Diffusion of Innovation model. In such cases, product adoption can rapidly spread across all customer segments, regardless of their typical characteristics.

"Introducing your innovation too early is like bringing sunscreen to a snowstorm - you're prepared, but nobody needs it!"

Several key elements contribute to perfect timing:

1. Market Readiness: A market that is primed and ready for a specific innovation can experience an unprecedented surge in adoption. If consumer needs align perfectly with what the innovation offers, adoption rates can escalate quickly.
2. Technological Advancements: Innovations that leverage recent technological advancements can gain a considerable advantage. When the technology is mature and affordable, early majority and late majority adopters may enter the scene simultaneously.
3. External Triggers: Events such as pandemics, regulatory changes, or economic shifts can alter the timing landscape. When an innovation

aligns with these external triggers, it can transcend the model's predictions.

An example of perfect timing can be seen in the rapid adoption of remote work technologies during the COVID-19 pandemic. These technologies traditionally belonged to the domain of early adopters but saw rapid adoption by the early majority and even the late majority due to the perfect timing of a global crisis.

Imperfect Timing: Disrupting the Model

Conversely, even when an innovation is meticulously designed and planned according to the Diffusion of Innovation model, imperfect timing can wreak havoc on the expected adoption rates. Several key elements are associated with imperfect timing:

1. Premature Entry: When an innovation enters the market before consumers are ready, it may be met with resistance. Early adopters might embrace it, but the early and late majority may remain skeptical.
2. Missed Opportunities: If an innovation misses a critical window of opportunity, adoption rates can suffer. Competing technologies or shifting market dynamics can affect the product's success.
3. Economic Conditions: Economic downturns can impede adoption, particularly among later adopter segments. Consumers may prioritize existing solutions over new innovations during uncertain economic times.

An example of imperfect timing can be found in the introduction of 3D television technology in the early 2010s. Despite its intriguing potential, it entered the market prematurely, and consumers were not prepared for the adoption leap it required.

Innovators need to assess market conditions carefully and customer needs to identify the optimal timing for their innovation's introduction. This may involve conducting market research, tracking emerging trends, and monitoring competitor activity.

By recognizing the role of timing and developing strategies to ensure optimal timing for their innovation's introduction, innovators can increase the likelihood of successful adoption and diffusion and the ultimate success of their innovation.

Six Degrees and Facebook — Six Degrees was the first social networking site launched in 1997. While it was ahead of its time in recognizing the potential of social networking, it failed to gain widespread adoption due to various factors, such as a lack of awareness, technical limitations, and the absence of a critical mass of users. As a result, it ultimately shut down in 2001, despite being the first mover in the social networking space.

In contrast, Facebook was launched in 2004, at a time when the internet and mobile technology had become more prevalent, and social networking had become a more established concept. Facebook built upon the lessons from early social networking pioneers like Six Degrees, Friendster, and MySpace and leveraged the existing infrastructure and user base to achieve rapid adoption and widespread diffusion.

Facebook's timing was critical to its success, as it was able to tap into a growing market demand for social networking while also addressing the limitations and challenges faced by earlier social networking sites. Its launch coincided with a shift in user behaviour towards sharing personal information and connecting with others online, making it an instant hit.

By recognizing the role of timing and adapting their innovation to market conditions and user needs, Facebook achieved successful adoption and diffusion. At the same time, Six Degrees struggled to gain traction due to timing and other factors.

09 The Role of User Experience

The role of user experience (UX) is a critical factor in the adoption and diffusion of innovations, often transcending the predictions of the Diffusion of Innovation model. User experience encompasses how individuals interact with an innovation and the overall satisfaction and delight they derive from using it. When an innovation offers a positive and seamless user experience, it is more likely to be adopted and diffused among users, cutting across traditional adopter categories. Conversely, if an innovation presents usability challenges or frustrations, it may face resistance or rejection, regardless of its potential benefits.

"Good UX is like a universal translator for innovation. It speaks the language of every adopter category, from Innovators to Laggards, and says, 'You've got this!'"

Understanding the Impact of User Experience:

1. **Ease of Use**: Innovations that are intuitive and easy to use are more likely to be embraced by users across different segments. When users find the technology or product straightforward, they are less deterred by the fear of complexity. This can lead to faster adoption, especially among those in the early and late majority.
2. **Minimizing Learning Curve**: Innovators that succeed in minimizing the learning curve for their innovations can expedite adoption. If users can quickly grasp how to use the product or technology, they are more inclined to adopt it. A shallow learning curve can be particularly appealing to the early and late majority.
3. **Effective Training and Support**: Providing adequate training and support resources can make a significant difference in adoption. When users have access to helpful guides, tutorials, or customer support, they

are more likely to overcome obstacles and continue using the innovation. This support can make a substantial impact on late majority and laggard segments.

4. **Feedback Integration**: Incorporating feedback from early adopters and users can refine the user experience. Early adopters, with their enthusiasm and willingness to provide input, can be valuable resources for improving the innovation. Addressing their feedback ensures that the technology or product aligns better with user expectations, which can boost adoption.

5. **Positive Word-of-Mouth and Social Influence**: A positive user experience can lead to organic word-of-mouth recommendations and social influence. When users have a delightful experience with an innovation, they are more likely to share it with their network and recommend it to others. This can lead to the rapid spread of the innovation, influencing segments beyond early adopters.

Examples of User Experience Impact:

1. **Smartphones**: The ease of use and intuitive interfaces of smartphones have played a substantial role in transcending traditional adoption patterns. Users of various backgrounds and demographics adopted smartphones more rapidly due to the positive user experience they provided.

2. **Social Media Platforms**: Platforms like Facebook and Instagram gained widespread adoption in part because they offered user-friendly interfaces and delightful experiences. This led to early and late majority segments embracing these innovations.

3. **Online Shopping**: E-commerce platforms that simplified the online shopping experience, offered user-friendly interfaces, and provided excellent customer support broke through traditional adoption barriers. Late majority users became comfortable with online shopping due to the positive user experience.

4. **Streaming Services**: The rise of streaming services such as Netflix can

be attributed to their user-friendly platforms and minimal learning curves. Users quickly adapted to this innovation, and it penetrated various adopter categories.

By recognizing the pivotal role of user experience and investing in strategies to enhance it, innovators can significantly increase the likelihood of successful adoption and diffusion of their innovations. A seamless, user-centric approach can enable innovations to transcend traditional adopter categories and gain traction more rapidly in the market.

"When an innovation offers a great user experience, it's like a catchy song you can't get out of your head - you want more of it!"

iPod: The advent of the iPod is a remarkable case study on how user experience can render the Diffusion of Innovation model irrelevant by drastically altering adoption rates. In the early 2000s, the market was flooded with various MP3 players, many of which offered similar features and functionalities. However, these products struggled to gain significant adoption, despite concerted branding and marketing efforts. Then came the iPod, which revolutionized the way people interacted with portable music players, transcending traditional adoption patterns.

Here's how the iPod, along with its ecosystem, redefined user experience and, in the process, made the Diffusion of Innovation model practically obsolete:

1. **Intuitive Navigation - The Scroll Wheel**: The iPod's iconic scroll wheel provided a simple and intuitive way to navigate through song lists. While other MP3 players relied on buttons, the scroll wheel made it easy to browse and select songs, appealing to a broad audience, including the early majority.

2. **Seamless Integration with iTunes**: Apple's iTunes software facilitated the effortless transfer of songs from a computer to the iPod. The intuitive interface of iTunes made it easier for users to manage their music libraries and synchronize them with the device, reducing barriers for the late majority.

3. **Streamlined User Interface**: Unlike many competing MP3 players with cluttered screens and numerous features, the iPod maintained a clean and minimalist interface. It displayed only the most frequently used functions, making it less intimidating for the late majority and laggards.

4. **Access to Any Song in a Few Clicks**: With a simple and user-friendly interface, accessing any song on the iPod took minimal effort and time. This streamlined user experience removed the complexity associated with early MP3 players, enticing the early and late majority to adopt the technology.

5. **The iTunes Store**: The introduction of the iTunes Store further transformed the music industry and iPod adoption. Users could easily purchase and download songs, integrating them seamlessly with their existing music libraries.

6. **Compact and Aesthetically Pleasing Design**: The iPod's sleek and compact design appealed to a wide range of users. It was not only a functional device but also a fashion statement. The early and late majority segments, influenced by aesthetics, found this aspect particularly compelling.

7. **Brand Ecosystem**: Apple's ecosystem approach played a significant role. iPods were designed to work seamlessly with Mac computers, creating a sense of desirability among existing Apple users and converting them into early majority adopters.

8. **Effective Marketing and Branding**: Apple's marketing and branding efforts capitalized on these user experience features, highlighting the simplicity and elegance of the iPod. This approach appealed to a broad audience, including the late majority.

The result of this user-centric approach was a surge in adoption that defied the traditional Diffusion of Innovation model. The iPod's user experience made it accessible and desirable across all adopter categories, rendering the model's predictions obsolete. Apple's focus on user-friendly design and intuitive interfaces set a new standard for the industry and exemplified how prioritizing user experience can lead to rapid and widespread adoption, making the diffusion model a relic of the past.

10 The Role of Competition

Competition in the marketplace can significantly disrupt this Diffusion of Innovation Model and lead to rapid and widespread adoption that defies its predictions. Here's a detailed explanation of how competition can make the Diffusion of Innovation model obsolete:

1. **Consumer Choice and Variety**: Competition in the market results in a variety of similar products or innovations. Consumers have choices, and they can quickly compare and contrast different offerings. This choice empowers consumers and accelerates adoption as they can select the innovation that best suits their needs.
2. **Faster Product Development**: In competitive industries, companies are motivated to innovate and develop products more quickly. This accelerated innovation cycle can lead to the introduction of new, improved versions of innovations, which can attract adopters from various segments.
3. **Price Competition**: Competing companies often engage in price wars to attract customers. Lower prices can make innovations more accessible, particularly to price-sensitive segments like the late majority and laggards, speeding up their adoption.
4. **Feature Enhancements**: To outdo their competitors, companies add features and capabilities to their innovations. This constant enhancement can increase the appeal of the innovation across different adopter categories, including the early and late majority.

5. **Marketing and Advertising**: Competition leads to more aggressive marketing and advertising efforts. Companies work harder to capture the attention of potential adopters. This can lead to higher awareness, interest, and, ultimately, adoption rates, even among traditionally slower segments.

6. **Compatibility and Interoperability**: Competition can lead to more standardization and efforts to ensure that innovations are compatible with one another. When innovations are interoperable, adopters from different segments find it easier to integrate them into their existing systems, leading to broader adoption.

7. **Network Effects**: In highly competitive markets, the presence of multiple products or innovations can create network effects. When an innovation becomes popular, the network effect can lead to rapid adoption as others join the same network, regardless of their adopter category.

8. **Rapid Adoption Cycles**: In competitive industries, adoption cycles can be shorter, with innovations moving from early adopters to laggards at an accelerated pace. Companies strive to outpace their competitors, resulting in quicker diffusion.

9. **Innovative Pricing Models**: To gain a competitive edge, companies might introduce innovative pricing models such as subscription services or freemium offerings. These models can attract adopters across different segments, especially if they offer value and convenience.

10. **Product Reviews and Recommendations**: In competitive markets, consumers often rely on product reviews, recommendations, and comparisons. Positive feedback and endorsements can sway potential adopters, leading to faster adoption.

11. **Chasing Market Share**: Companies are often in a race to capture a larger share of the market. This aggressive pursuit can result in strategies aimed at reaching the entire population, not just early adopters.

Competition can also create barriers to adoption and diffusion. Potential adopters may be overwhelmed by a crowded marketplace or hesitant to switch to innovation if they are satisfied with existing products. Competing innovations may also create confusion or fragmentation in the market, making it more difficult for innovators to gain a foothold and achieve widespread adoption and diffusion.

"When competition heats up, innovation adoption turns into a game of musical chairs. Just hope you're not left standing with outdated technology!"

Smartphones: Let's consider the smartphone market, particularly the competition between Apple's iPhone and various Android-based devices. The introduction and evolution of smartphones have drastically altered the adoption landscape, challenging the traditional Diffusion of Innovation model.

1. Consumer Choice and Variety: The smartphone market offers a plethora of choices, with various manufacturers producing devices running on the Android operating system. Consumers can choose from an array of brands, models, and features, allowing them to select the device that best aligns with their preferences and needs.

2. Faster Product Development: Intense competition in the smartphone industry drives rapid product development. Manufacturers are continuously innovating, introducing new features, and improving existing ones. This rapid innovation encourages early adopters to upgrade to the latest devices while also attracting the attention of the early and late majority.

3. Price Competition: Price wars are common in the smartphone market. As manufacturers compete for market share, they often lower prices to attract a broader customer base. Lower prices make smartphones more accessible, accelerating adoption among price-sensitive consumers in the late majority and laggard segments.

4. Feature Enhancements: Features such as larger screens, better cameras, and improved processing power are introduced regularly to outdo competitors.

These enhancements increase the appeal of smartphones across various adopter categories.

5. Marketing and Advertising: Apple and Android device manufacturers engage in extensive marketing and advertising campaigns. These efforts raise awareness and generate interest among potential adopters across all segments.

6. Compatibility and Interoperability: Both Apple and Android smartphones have worked on compatibility and interoperability, allowing users to switch between devices or adopt multiple devices within the same ecosystem. This compatibility encourages adoption by removing barriers related to transitioning from one brand to another.

7. Network Effects: The widespread adoption of smartphones, whether iOS or Android-based, has created network effects. The more people use a particular type of smartphone, the more valuable it becomes due to app compatibility, social communication, and other network-related benefits. This dynamic can lead to rapid adoption by individuals who wish to be part of the same network, regardless of their adopter category.

8. Rapid Adoption Cycles: In the smartphone market, the adoption cycle from early adopters to laggards can be relatively short. Early adopters eagerly embrace new models, but the quick pace of innovation means that innovations, once adopted by early adopters, soon become standard features, making them appealing to a wider audience.

9. Innovative Pricing Models: Both Apple and Android device manufacturers offer innovative pricing models, such as trade-in programs, financing, and subscription services. These models make smartphones more affordable and attainable for a broader range of consumers.

10. Product Reviews and Recommendations: Consumers often rely on product reviews, recommendations, and comparisons to make their smartphone choices. Positive reviews and endorsements from early adopters or influencers can influence potential adopters, further accelerating adoption.

11. Chasing Market Share: Apple and Android manufacturers aggressively pursue market share. They aim to reach the entire population, focusing on extensive distribution and accessibility, rather than solely targeting early adopters.

In this highly competitive context, the traditional Diffusion of Innovation model doesn't accurately capture the dynamics of smartphone adoption. The model's linear progression from innovators to laggards is disrupted, and instead, we see rapid, nonlinear adoption across various segments. The choice, competition, rapid product evolution, and extensive marketing campaigns have made the smartphone market a prime example of how competition can render the traditional diffusion model obsolete.

Apple vs Microsoft: The competition between Microsoft and Apple in their earlier years is a classic example of how competition can drive rapid product adoption and make the traditional Diffusion of Innovation model less relevant.

1. **Personal Computers (PCs):** In the late 1970s and early 1980s, both Microsoft and Apple were pioneers in the personal computer industry. Microsoft's operating system, MS-DOS, and Apple's Macintosh were competing platforms. This rivalry accelerated the adoption of personal computers across various customer segments.

2. **User-Friendly Interfaces:** Apple's Macintosh introduced a graphical user interface (GUI), making personal computers more accessible to non-technical users. This innovation influenced Microsoft to develop Windows, which also offered a GUI. The user-friendly interfaces of both systems appealed to early and late majority adopters.

3. **Business vs. Creative Use:** Microsoft and Apple targeted different customer segments initially. Microsoft focused on business users with MS-DOS and Windows, while Apple positioned itself as the choice for creative professionals with Macintosh. This diverse targeting expanded the adoption of personal computers across multiple segments.

4. **Software Compatibility:** Competition between the two companies led to the development of various software applications, further fueling PC adoption. Microsoft's Office Suite and Apple's software for creative professionals, like Adobe's products, became essential tools for different user groups.

5. **Ecosystem Development:** Both companies invested in developing ecosystems around their platforms. Microsoft's ecosystem included partner-

ships with various hardware manufacturers, while Apple tightly controlled both hardware and software. This competition drove innovations and the expansion of ecosystems, attracting users from early to late adopter categories.

6. Marketing and Advertising: Microsoft and Apple engaged in vigorous marketing campaigns. Apple's famous "1984" Super Bowl commercial and Microsoft's "Where do you want to go today?" campaign are examples. These efforts raised awareness and created interest among consumers.

7. Rapid Product Iteration: The competition between Microsoft and Apple pushed both companies to iterate rapidly. Each new version of their operating systems or hardware products introduced innovations that attracted different segments of users, from early adopters to the late majority.

8. Compatibility and Interoperability: As competition intensified, both companies worked to improve compatibility and interoperability with other systems and devices. This made transitioning between Microsoft and Apple products more seamless, contributing to the adoption of both platforms.

9. Shifts in Market Share: Microsoft and Apple have experienced shifts in market share over the years. This competition has driven constant innovation and efforts to recapture or expand market share. These shifts have led to the adoption of products and technologies by different customer segments.

10. Leveraging Third-Party Developers: Both Microsoft and Apple encouraged third-party developers to create software for their platforms. This increased the variety of applications available, attracting users from different segments.

In summary, the competition between Microsoft and Apple in the personal computer industry's early years significantly impacted product adoption. The competitive landscape spurred innovation, rapid product development, and diverse targeting strategies that led to the rapid adoption of personal computers, making the traditional Diffusion of Innovation model less relevant in this context. This competition ultimately contributed to the widespread use of personal computers across various customer segments.

Coke vs Pepsi: Competition often plays a crucial role in popularizing a product category and driving adoption, rendering the traditional Diffusion of Innovation model less relevant. A prime example of this phenomenon can be observed in the competition between industry giants, Coca–Cola (Coke) and PepsiCo (Pepsi), in the soft drink industry.

1. Advertising and Marketing Wars: Coca–Cola and Pepsi have engaged in legendary advertising and marketing battles for decades. Their relentless competition has led to a substantial increase in advertising spending, not just for their own brands but for the soft drink category as a whole. These marketing efforts have included memorable ad campaigns, sponsorships, and endorsements, which have garnered significant public attention.

2. Brand Differentiation: While both companies essentially sell similar carbonated beverages, their marketing strategies focus on differentiating their brands. Coke positions itself as the classic choice, emphasizing heritage and nostalgia. In contrast, Pepsi often portrays itself as the choice of a younger generation, emphasizing innovation and a "Pepsi Generation" lifestyle. This brand differentiation has expanded the appeal of soft drinks to diverse customer segments.

3. Broadening the Appeal: The intense competition between Coke and Pepsi has led to the creation of numerous beverage variations and flavors to cater to different tastes. This diversification broadens the appeal of soft drinks, making them relevant to a wide range of consumers, from early adopters to the late majority.

4. Market Entry and Expansion: The competition between these giants has driven market entry and expansion. Their marketing efforts have often included global campaigns, entering new markets and introducing soft drinks to consumers who may have never considered them before. This has expanded the reach of the product category.

5. Pricing and Promotions: Competitive pricing and promotions are another aspect of the battle between Coke and Pepsi. Price wars, special promotions, and limited–time offerings have created a sense of urgency and excitement around soft drinks. Consumers across various adoption stages are enticed by these deals.

6. Increased Product Visibility: The rivalry between the two companies has led to widespread product visibility. Soft drink vending machines, advertisements, and promotions are ubiquitous, ensuring that potential adopters from various segments are continually exposed to these products.

In summary, the competition between Coca-Cola and PepsiCo in the soft drink industry has played a pivotal role in popularizing the soft drink category and driving adoption. The extensive advertising and marketing wars, coupled with brand differentiation, broadened product appeal, and market entry, have expanded the category's reach and rendered the traditional Diffusion of Innovation model less relevant. Instead of following a linear adoption curve, the competition has created a dynamic and ever-evolving landscape where more people are exposed to and inclined to try soft drinks, leading to increased product adoption.

Uber vs Lyft: The competition between Uber and Lyft in the ride-sharing industry provides another example of how rivalry can drive the popularization of a service and rapidly increase adoption and diffusion, rendering traditional models, like the Diffusion of Innovation, less relevant.

1. **Introduction of a New Concept:** Ride-sharing was a relatively new concept when Uber and Lyft entered the market. Their innovative approach to transportation services disrupted traditional taxi and car rental services. The idea of using a smartphone app to request rides from ordinary drivers was unfamiliar to many consumers.

2. **Aggressive Marketing and Promotion:** Uber and Lyft engaged in aggressive marketing and promotion to outdo each other. This competition led to substantial investments in advertising, which not only promoted their individual services but popularized the entire concept of ride-sharing.

3. **Competitive Pricing:** Both companies continuously adjusted their pricing strategies in response to each other's actions. Price wars, discounts, and promotions became common in the industry, making ride-sharing more affordable and appealing to a broad range of customers.

4. **Innovation and Product Differentiation:** The competition fueled innovation in the industry. Features like carpooling, shared rides, luxury car services, and food delivery were introduced to attract a diverse customer

base. These innovations expanded the appeal of ride-sharing beyond early adopters.

5. Expanding Market Reach: Uber and Lyft's rivalry led to rapid expansion into various cities and countries. This geographical expansion meant that more people were exposed to the concept of ride-sharing, regardless of their location or socio-economic status.

6. Customer Referral Programs: Both companies introduced referral programs that rewarded customers for referring friends and family. These programs helped generate positive word-of-mouth and social influence, driving more individuals to try ride-sharing.

7. App User Experience: Uber and Lyft invested heavily in app development, making the user experience simple, convenient, and enjoyable. Users could easily request rides, track drivers, and make cashless payments, which contributed to higher satisfaction and adoption rates.

8. Regulatory Challenges: The competition between Uber and Lyft often extended to regulatory challenges in various markets. These challenges resulted in public discussions and media coverage, bringing even more attention to ride-sharing and increasing consumer awareness.

9. Service Improvements: Competition spurred service improvements. Both companies worked to address user feedback, enhance driver training, and improve safety measures. These improvements increased trust and adoption.

10. Positive Feedback Loop: The intense competition created a positive feedback loop. As more people adopted ride-sharing, the services became more accessible, reliable, and affordable. This, in turn, attracted more customers.

In summary, the intense competition between Uber and Lyft in the ride-sharing industry popularized the concept and rapidly increased the adoption and diffusion of these services.

11 The Role of Infrastructure

Infrastructure is a fundamental yet often overlooked factor that significantly influences the adoption and diffusion of innovations. The Diffusion of Innovation model, while valuable in understanding the behavioural aspects of adoption, often fails to consider the critical role that infrastructure plays in the successful integration of innovations into various contexts. Let's delve into the importance of infrastructure in the adoption and diffusion of innovations.

1. **Technological Infrastructure:** Technological infrastructure encompasses the hardware, software, and networks necessary for innovations to function effectively. Without compatible and reliable infrastructure, innovations may struggle to gain traction. For example, the adoption of electric vehicles relies on the availability of charging stations, making infrastructure a key determinant of their success.

2. **Communication Networks:** The accessibility and quality of communication networks, including the internet and mobile connectivity, significantly impact how innovations spread. In regions with limited or unreliable network coverage, the adoption of digital innovations, such as online education platforms or telehealth services, may be impeded.

3. **Transportation and Logistics Infrastructure:** The ability to transport and distribute goods and services affects innovation adoption. For instance, the success of food delivery apps relies on the existence of efficient transportation and delivery infrastructure.

4. **Energy and Utility Infrastructure:** Innovations related to renewable energy, like solar panels or wind turbines, are contingent on the availability of a robust energy infrastructure. Without the necessary infrastructure to connect these energy sources to the grid, their adoption is hindered.

5. **Healthcare Infrastructure:** The healthcare sector's capacity to adopt medical innovations depends on its infrastructure, including hospitals, clinics, and medical equipment. The adoption of new medical technologies is limited by the availability of these resources.

6. **Educational Infrastructure:** Innovations in education, such as e-learning platforms, require suitable educational infrastructure, including

schools, classrooms, and internet connectivity. Inadequate infrastructure can impede students' access to these innovations.

7. Regulatory and Legal Infrastructure: Legal frameworks and regulatory infrastructure are critical for innovations like autonomous vehicles or fintech solutions. Inconsistent or outdated regulations can hinder the adoption of such innovations.

8. Public Infrastructure Investment: Government investments in public infrastructure, such as smart cities, can facilitate the integration of innovations into urban environments. These investments can create environments that are more conducive to the rapid adoption of innovative technologies and services.

9. Environmental Infrastructure: Innovations targeting environmental sustainability, such as waste management solutions or urban farming, depend on the environmental infrastructure of a region. The lack of recycling facilities, for example, can hinder the adoption of recycling innovations.

10. Supply Chain Infrastructure: Innovations in supply chain management and logistics benefit from an efficient supply chain infrastructure. This is particularly relevant for innovations that aim to streamline the movement of goods and reduce operational costs.

In summary, the role of infrastructure in the adoption and diffusion of innovations cannot be overstated. It is the underlying support system that enables innovations to thrive within specific contexts. Without appropriate infrastructure, even the most promising innovations may struggle to gain widespread adoption. For a more comprehensive understanding of innovation diffusion, it is essential to consider the interplay between behavioural factors and the supporting infrastructure, as they collectively shape the trajectory of innovation adoption. The Diffusion of Innovation model's focus on individual and social aspects of adoption needs to be complemented with a consideration of infrastructure to provide a more holistic view of the adoption process.

"In the innovation race, infrastructure is the pit stop that keeps everyone going. Without it, you'd be stuck in the slow lane forever!"

Online Streaming Services: Online streaming services, offering movies and TV shows over the internet, represent a significant innovation in the entertainment industry. One of the pioneers in this space is Netflix. However, their successful adoption was not solely driven by the innovative nature of the service but was highly dependent on the existing infrastructure.

1. Technological Infrastructure: Online streaming services rely heavily on technological infrastructure, especially high-speed internet. In the early 2000s, when Netflix started its streaming service, high-speed broadband internet was not as widespread as it is today. This limited the potential user base for streaming services. In areas with slow or unreliable internet connections, the user experience was poor, and streaming was often not feasible.

2. Communication Networks: The quality of communication networks played a pivotal role in the diffusion of online streaming. The availability of fast and reliable internet connections was essential for users to stream content without interruptions. Areas with inadequate network infrastructure saw slower adoption of these services.

3. Content Delivery Infrastructure: A critical part of online streaming is content delivery networks (CDNs). CDNs are responsible for efficiently delivering content to users. Netflix invested significantly in building its CDN, known as Open Connect. This infrastructure was designed to reduce the load on the broader internet and provide smoother streaming experiences. It allowed Netflix to maintain high-quality streaming even in areas with less developed internet infrastructure.

4. Device Compatibility: The adoption of streaming services was also influenced by the device compatibility infrastructure. The availability of smart TVs, gaming consoles, and streaming devices (like Roku or Amazon Fire TV) made it easier for users to access streaming content on their televisions. This compatibility infrastructure accelerated adoption.

5. Legal and Regulatory Infrastructure: Netflix and other streaming services had to navigate complex copyright and licensing regulations. The legal and regulatory infrastructure influenced what content could be offered in different regions and how it was accessed.

6. Public Awareness: Infrastructure isn't limited to physical elements. Public awareness campaigns and education about streaming services contributed to their adoption. This information infrastructure was essential for users to understand the benefits and convenience of online streaming.

7. Investment in Original Content: Another aspect of infrastructure was Netflix's investment in original content. This strategic infrastructure decision set Netflix apart and attracted subscribers. By producing original series and movies, they ensured they had a unique offering compared to traditional cable TV.

Netflix's success in the adoption of online streaming services was not solely due to the novelty of the service. It was deeply entwined with the state of infrastructure – whether it was the quality of internet connections, content delivery, device compatibility, legal frameworks, public awareness, or investment in exclusive content. The traditional Diffusion of Innovation model may not fully capture the influence of infrastructure in this context, as it primarily focuses on the characteristics of individual users and their social networks. Therefore, understanding the role of infrastructure provides a more comprehensive picture of how innovations are adopted and diffused in real-world scenarios.

12 The Role of Network Effects

The Diffusion of Innovation model has been a valuable framework for understanding how new ideas, products, or technologies spread through a population. However, it often doesn't adequately account for the role of network effects, which can significantly impact adoption rates and render the traditional model less relevant.

Network effects occur when the value of a product or service increases as more people use it. In essence, the more individuals adopt the innovation, the more valuable it becomes for everyone. This dynamic is particularly relevant in the digital age, where connectivity and network-based platforms play a central role in innovation diffusion.

Impact of Network Effects on Innovation Adoption:

1. **Rapid Adoption Acceleration:** Network effects can lead to rapid and exponential adoption. As more users join a network, there is an incentive for others to follow suit to reap the benefits of network participation. This can lead to a "tipping point" where adoption accelerates significantly, and the model's gradual progression may not apply.

2. **Non-Linear Growth:** Network effects often result in non-linear growth patterns. Instead of a steady progression from innovators to early adopters, early majority, late majority, and laggards, you might see a quick transition from innovators to early and late majorities as the network effect kicks in.

3. **Cross-Segment Adoption:** Network effects can break down traditional segmentation. In the context of network-based innovations, early adopters might include both tech-savvy individuals and entire organizations that recognize the benefits of network participation. This cross-segment adoption challenges the model's assumption of distinct adopter categories.

Examples of Network Effects Impacting Adoption:

1. **Social Media Platforms:** Social media networks like Facebook and Twitter are classic examples of network effects. The more users these platforms have, the more valuable they become. Their adoption rates skyrocketed due to these effects, with individuals, businesses, and even governments participating. This rapid and non-linear adoption doesn't

align with the traditional model's predictions.

2. **Ride-Sharing Services:** Uber and Lyft disrupted the transportation industry through network effects. As more riders joined, the services became more efficient and widely available, attracting even more riders. The model's progression from early to late majority wasn't as linear as expected.

3. **Online Marketplaces:** Platforms like Amazon and eBay are characterized by network effects. As more sellers join, there are more products for buyers to choose from, attracting more buyers. This interplay between buyers and sellers led to rapid and non-linear adoption.

4. **Messaging Apps:** Apps like WhatsApp and WeChat have seen staggering adoption rates due to network effects. Once a user's contacts join the same platform, it becomes their preferred communication channel. The influence of network effects is evident in the swift adoption across different user segments.

Network effects can render the Diffusion of Innovation model less relevant by creating adoption patterns that deviate from the model's predictions. When innovations thrive on the connections and interactions among users, it's crucial to consider network effects and their potential to drive rapid, non-linear, and cross-segment adoption.

Amazon and Network Effects: Amazon's growth and widespread adoption have defied the traditional Diffusion of Innovation model due to these network effects.

1. **Marketplace Expansion:** Amazon began as an online bookseller, but it quickly expanded into various product categories. As more third-party sellers joined the platform, offering a broader range of products, the value of Amazon increased for customers. This expansion attracted more buyers to the platform, leading to rapid and non-linear adoption.

2. **Amazon Prime:** Amazon introduced Amazon Prime, a subscription service offering free and fast shipping, access to streaming services,

and more. As more customers subscribed to Prime, the benefits of membership, such as free shipping and exclusive content, became more valuable. This prompted a significant surge in Prime subscriptions and Amazon adoption, as customers saw the value of being part of the network.

3. **User Reviews and Recommendations:** Amazon's user review and recommendation systems have been integral to its success. As more customers left reviews and ratings, the platform's value for prospective buyers increased. Shoppers could make informed decisions based on the experiences of others, which further accelerated adoption.

4. **Seller Services:** Amazon offers a range of services for sellers, including fulfillment services, advertising, and access to its customer base. As more sellers leveraged these services and reached a wider audience, the platform attracted an increasing number of merchants and products. This dynamic network of buyers and sellers led to Amazon's dominance in the e-commerce market.

5. **Echo and Alexa:** Amazon's smart devices, including Echo and Alexa, are part of a broader ecosystem. As more consumers adopted these devices, the value of owning them increased due to their interconnected capabilities. This encouraged more people to incorporate these devices into their homes.

Amazon's adoption curve doesn't align with the traditional Diffusion of Innovation model. The rapid expansion and adoption across various customer segments, from early adopters to laggards, are largely driven by the network effects created by the platform. As more users and sellers joined the network, the value of Amazon grew for all participants, leading to exponential and non-linear adoption. This phenomenon has reshaped e-commerce and retail, making the model less relevant in Amazon's case.

13 Challenging the Categories

One of the limitations of the Diffusion of Innovation model is the challenge of categorizing people into discrete groups like Innovators, Early Adopters, Early Majority, Late Majority, and Laggards. While the model has been influential and useful in understanding the general patterns of adoption, it oversimplifies the complexity of human behaviour and the adoption process.

"The Diffusion of Innovation model makes it sound like people come with a barcode that says 'Innovator' or 'Laggard.' But in reality, we're more like a box of assorted chocolates - you never know what you're gonna get!

Here's why this categorization has limitations:

1. **Fluidity of Adoption Behavior:** Human behavior is not static, and people do not fit neatly into predefined categories. The model assumes that individuals consistently belong to one category across all innovations. In reality, individuals can exhibit different adoption behaviors for various innovations, depending on factors like their perception of the innovation's value, their familiarity with the technology, and the specific context.

2. **Contextual Factors:** The model does not adequately account for contextual factors that can influence adoption behavior. Different innovations may require unique contextual considerations. For example, a person who is generally an Early Adopter for technology-related innovations may exhibit Late Majority behavior when it comes to healthcare innovations due to personal health concerns.

3. **Varying Perceptions of Risk:** The model simplifies the role of risk perception. It assumes that Laggards are inherently more risk-averse, while Early Adopters are more risk-tolerant. However, the perceived risks associated with an innovation can vary greatly based on factors

such as the individual's prior experiences, the consequences of failure, and the novelty of the technology.

4. **Changing Technologies and Social Norms:** As technology and societal norms evolve, so does adoption behavior. Someone who was once considered a Laggard for adopting smartphones may later become an Early Majority adopter for a different technology, reflecting the changing landscape and social acceptance.

5. **Individual Differences:** The model does not consider the vast individual differences that can influence adoption. Personal preferences, values, and motivations can lead individuals to make choices that do not align with their typical categorization.

6. **Cultural and Demographic Variations:** Cultural, demographic, and geographical factors can significantly impact adoption behavior. What is considered innovative or acceptable can differ from one culture or region to another. The model does not address these variations comprehensively.

7. **Cross-Cutting Innovations:** In some cases, an innovation may not neatly fit into the traditional categorization. It might have features that appeal to both Early Adopters and the Early Majority, creating a more complex adoption pattern.

8. **Time Sensitivity:** The model implies a linear progression from Innovators to Laggards over time. However, this does not account for the fact that innovations can rapidly spread through social networks, leading to non-linear adoption curves.

To address these limitations, it's important to recognize the fluid and dynamic nature of adoption behavior. Rather than adhering strictly to predefined categories, innovators and marketers should consider a more nuanced approach. This approach involves conducting detailed market research, understanding the specific factors influencing adoption for a particular innovation, and tailoring strategies accordingly. The goal is to account for the complexity of individual behavior and create adoption pathways that resonate with the diverse needs and perceptions of potential adopters.

14 The Role of Cognitive Biases

The role of cognitive biases in influencing adoption rates is a fascinating aspect that the traditional Diffusion of Innovation model does not explicitly consider. Cognitive biases are systematic patterns of deviation from norm or rationality in judgment, often leading individuals to make decisions in predictable but irrational ways. Companies can leverage these biases to increase adoption rates and transcend traditional adopter categories. Let's explore some of these cognitive biases and how they can impact innovation adoption:

1. **Scarcity Bias:** Scarcity bias occurs when people place a higher value on things that are perceived as scarce or in limited supply. Companies can use this bias to create a sense of urgency or exclusivity around their innovations. Limited-time offers, exclusive memberships, or product scarcity can drive rapid adoption, as people fear missing out on a valuable opportunity. *Example*: A software company introduces a limited-time offer for its premium features at a discounted price, creating a sense of scarcity. As a result, adoption rates spike as people rush to take advantage of the deal.

2. **Authority Bias:** People tend to follow the lead of credible and authoritative figures. Companies can leverage this bias by involving authoritative figures or experts to endorse or recommend their innovation. Such endorsements can significantly influence adoption rates, even among skeptics. *Example*: A health tech startup partners with renowned medical professionals who endorse their health monitoring app. The authoritative endorsements lend credibility to the app, encouraging even skeptics to adopt it.

3. **Confirmation Bias:** Confirmation bias is the tendency to search for, interpret, and remember information that confirms one's preconceptions. Companies can utilize this bias by crafting marketing and messaging that aligns with users' existing beliefs and preferences, making the innovation more appealing. *Example*: A political news app tailors

content recommendations based on a user's past reading habits and political preferences, reinforcing their existing beliefs and increasing app adoption.

4. **Recency Bias:** This bias leads people to give more weight to recent events and information. Companies can use this bias to create a perception of novelty and relevance for their innovation, attracting a broader audience. *Example*: A mobile phone manufacturer continually releases new models with minor updates. Customers, influenced by the recency bias, opt for the latest model, driving rapid adoption among different adopter categories.

5. **Social Proof Bias:** Social proof is the tendency to adopt the behavior or opinions of a group. Companies can leverage social proof by showcasing user testimonials, reviews, and endorsements to create a bandwagon effect, prompting potential adopters to follow suit. *Example*: A restaurant app highlights user reviews and ratings for various restaurants. As more users flock to the highly-rated eateries, others follow, significantly increasing the app's adoption.

6. **Anchoring Bias:** Anchoring bias occurs when people rely heavily on the first piece of information encountered (the "anchor") when making decisions. Companies can use anchoring to set a favorable reference point for the innovation's value, thereby influencing adoption decisions. *Example*: An e-commerce platform presents a high original price for a product and then offers it at a discounted price. Customers anchor on the original price, perceiving the discount as a significant deal, leading to increased adoption.

Leveraging cognitive biases in marketing and product design can indeed lead to the rapid adoption of innovations, often transcending the boundaries of traditional adopter categories. Understanding these biases and using them ethically can be a powerful tool for companies seeking to promote their innovations effectively.

15 The Role of Event-driven Adoption

The diffusion of innovation model largely ignores the profound influence of major events and occasions that can dramatically reshape adoption patterns.

Event-driven adoption pertains to the strategic use of major events, occasions, or milestones to stimulate consumer interest, excitement, and engagement, thereby propelling the adoption of innovations. These events could range from global occurrences such as the Olympic Games or World Cup to more localized events like cultural festivals, holidays, or even product launches.

"Launching an innovation at the right event is like telling a perfectly timed joke. It gets a laugh, a nod, and maybe even a standing ovation!

Key Elements of Event-driven Adoption

1. **Heightened Consumer Engagement:** Major events and occasions naturally capture public attention and generate heightened engagement. People are more receptive to new ideas and innovations during these periods.
2. **Emotional Connection:** Events often evoke strong emotions, and businesses can capitalize on this to create memorable experiences that encourage innovation adoption.
3. **Contextual Relevance:** Effective event-driven adoption is rooted in the context of the occasion. Innovations should align with the event's theme, purpose, or the specific needs and desires of the audience during that time.
4. **Timeliness:** Timing is crucial. Businesses must launch their innovations or campaigns in sync with the event to maximize the impact.

Examples of Event-driven Adoption

1. **Olympic Games and Sports Brands:** The Olympic Games are a global phenomenon, and sports brands often leverage this event to launch innovative products like athletic gear and equipment. The Games create a fervor for sports and athleticism, making it an opportune moment to introduce new sports-related innovations.
2. **Holiday Seasons and Retail:** During holiday seasons, retailers introduce various sales and promotions, offering consumers innovative products or services as gifts or for personal use. The emotional and festive context enhances the adoption of these innovations.
3. **Apple's iPhone Launches:** Apple has masterfully used product launches as events. People eagerly anticipate new iPhone releases, and Apple capitalizes on this by introducing innovative features and technologies during these events. This approach drastically accelerates adoption across consumer segments.
4. **Movie Releases and Merchandise:** Film studios release merchandise tied to major movie launches, leveraging the excitement generated by these events. Innovative toys, clothing, and collectibles related to popular movies experience rapid adoption.

Event-driven adoption reshapes innovation adoption patterns, often sidestepping the traditional diffusion of innovation model. Major events and occasions provide an extraordinary platform for businesses to engage consumers, elicit emotional connections, and drive rapid adoption of their innovations.

16 The Role of Branding and Association

The Role of Branding and Association is a paramount factor in understanding how innovations can transcend the traditional linear curve of the Diffusion of Innovation model. This factor sheds light on the profound influence of brand identity and consumer perceptions in driving the rapid adoption and diffusion of innovations. When innovations are introduced by well-known brands with which customers have positive associations, they can break free from the linear model's constraints and achieve widespread adoption across diverse consumer segments.

The Power of Brand Identity:

1. **Established Trust:** Well-known brands have already established trust and credibility among consumers. People tend to have preconceived notions about the quality, reliability, and consistency associated with such brands. This trust serves as a powerful foundation for the rapid adoption of innovations.
2. **Consumer Loyalty:** Customers often develop loyalty to brands that have consistently delivered positive experiences and products. These loyal customers are more inclined to adopt new offerings from the same brand, capitalizing on the positive associations they've formed over time.
3. **Emotional Connection:** Brands that have successfully cultivated emotional connections with consumers hold a unique advantage. When an innovation is introduced by such a brand, consumers are not just adopting a product; they are partaking in an experience that aligns with their emotions and values.

Consumer Perceptions and Associations:

1. **Brand Personality:** Consumers attribute personality traits to brands. These perceptions can include qualities like sophistication, reliability, or innovation. When an innovation mirrors the brand's established personality, consumers are more likely to embrace it.
2. **Heritage and Legacy:** Brands with a rich heritage and legacy can leverage their history to introduce innovations with a sense of authority and time-tested excellence. This can reassure consumers and expedite adoption.
3. **Positive Brand Experiences:** If customers have had consistently positive

experiences with a brand, they tend to associate this positivity with any new offerings from that brand. Innovations then benefit from this reservoir of goodwill.

Examples:

1. Apple Inc.: Apple is a quintessential example of a brand that has defied the traditional diffusion model. With each new product launch, Apple attracts a diverse consumer base. The company's strong brand identity, consumer loyalty, and the emotional connection it fosters have been instrumental in driving rapid adoption. Whether it's iPhones, iPads, or MacBooks, the Apple brand's positive associations with innovation, user-friendliness, and cutting-edge technology have led to non-linear adoption curves.

2. Coca-Cola: Coca-Cola's innovations in the beverage industry have consistently enjoyed rapid adoption. The brand's deep-rooted heritage, global recognition, and the positive memories consumers associate with its products have played a pivotal role. Coca-Cola's introduction of new flavors or limited editions taps into its brand power, and consumers across various segments quickly embrace these innovations.

3. Tesla: Tesla, an electric vehicle (EV) manufacturer, has redefined the automotive industry. The brand's association with sustainability, cutting-edge technology, and Elon Musk's vision has led to rapid EV adoption. Consumers who might not have considered EVs previously are now willing to make the switch due to Tesla's innovative approach and brand allure.

The Role of Branding and Association demonstrates that consumer perceptions and the power of established brands can significantly influence the rapid adoption and diffusion of innovations.

17 The Role of Identity Marketing

Identity Marketing is a compelling strategy that goes beyond traditional marketing approaches. It involves enabling customers to showcase and express their identity through the use of a product or service. This unique strategy is a game-changer in driving rapid innovation adoption, often making the Diffusion of Innovation model irrelevant. Identity Marketing empowers consumers to market themselves, creating a profound emotional connection between the consumer and the innovation.

"Traditional marketing asks, 'What can we sell you?' Identity Marketing asks, 'Who do you want to be today, and how can we help you become that superhero or unicorn?'"

- Identity Marketing revolves around the concept of self-expression. It recognizes that consumers seek products or services that resonate with their personal identity, values, and aspirations. Innovations that enable individuals to express their identity tend to experience rapid adoption.
- At the heart of Identity Marketing is the creation of a deep emotional connection. When consumers see an innovation as a means of expressing themselves, it transcends the transactional relationship and becomes an integral part of their identity.
- Identity Marketing prioritizes the user and their unique identity. It's not just about selling a product; it's about understanding the consumer's self-image, values, and how the product or service aligns with their sense of self.

Examples:

1. Nike: The Art of Identity Marketing: Nike, the sportswear giant, has mastered Identity Marketing. Their "Just Do It" campaign isn't just about selling sneakers; it's about empowering individuals to express their athletic identity. Nike's innovative products, coupled with compelling storytelling, resonate with consumers looking to embody a sporty, active, and determined identity. This approach has led to rapid adoption across various consumer segments.

2. Instagram: Instagram has become the epitome of Identity Marketing in the digital realm. The platform allows users to curate their visual identity through photos, stories, and captions. It's not merely a social network; it's a canvas for self-expression. Users adopt Instagram rapidly because it aligns with their need to showcase their identity, experiences, and interests.

18 Lack of Attention to Laggards

Another notable limitation of the Diffusion of Innovation Model is its lack of attention to the "Laggards" category.

The Diffusion of Innovation model categorizes the population into five groups based on their adoption behaviour: Innovators, Early Adopters, Early Majority, Late Majority, and Laggards. Laggards are typically characterized as individuals who are the last to adopt an innovation, often well after the majority of the population has already embraced it. They tend to be skeptical of new ideas and may exhibit resistance to change.

"Laggards are like the last slice of pizza at a party - often ignored, but sometimes the most satisfying bite."

Here are some key reasons why the model's lack of attention to Laggards is a limitation:

1. **Underrepresentation:** Laggards are the last group to be considered in the model, and their characteristics and behaviors are given less attention compared to other adopter categories. This underrepresentation can result in a one-sided view of the adoption process, focusing predominantly on the early and majority adopters.

2. **Influence on Adoption:** While Laggards may be slow to adopt innova-

tions, they still play a significant role in the adoption process. Ignoring this segment can lead to oversimplified predictions and strategies that do not account for the full spectrum of adopters.

3. **Stigmatization:** The term "Laggards" itself can carry a negative connotation, suggesting that these individuals are backward or resistant to progress. Such stigmatization can perpetuate biases and create a bias against this group, further marginalizing them.

4. **Unique Needs:** Laggards often have distinct needs and concerns that should not be overlooked. Their hesitancy to adopt innovations may stem from valid considerations, such as cost, risk, or compatibility with existing practices. Understanding these concerns is essential for innovators seeking to bridge the adoption gap.

5. **Unrealized Potential:** Laggards can represent an untapped market potential. By addressing their specific concerns and barriers to adoption, businesses and innovators can potentially accelerate the adoption of their innovations, thereby expanding their market reach.

6. **Variability:** Not all Laggards are the same. The model does not account for the variability within this category. Some may eventually adopt innovations when they see the benefits, while others may remain resistant for various reasons.

The lack of attention to Laggards in the Diffusion of Innovation model is a limitation because it overlooks an important segment of the population that plays a role in the adoption process. Recognizing the unique characteristics, needs, and potential of Laggards is crucial for a more comprehensive understanding of how innovations spread and for developing effective strategies to bridge the adoption gap.

19 Overshadowing Innovators and Early Adopters

The Diffusion of Innovation model's primary focus on later adopter categories can overshadow the critical role played by Innovators and Early Adopters in the innovation adoption process.

"It's as if the model only cares about the dessert (Early and Late Majority), ignoring the appetizers (Innovators and Early Adopters) that make the meal worth savoring."

This limitation occurs for several reasons:

1. **Marginalized Influence:** The model allocates minimal attention to Innovators and Early Adopters as they represent a smaller portion of the population. Instead, it emphasizes the larger segments, the Early Majority and the Late Majority. While these later adopter categories are essential for widespread adoption, it's the Innovators and Early Adopters who kickstart the process.

2. **Early Momentum:** Innovators and Early Adopters are instrumental in initiating momentum for an innovation. They are often the first to embrace new ideas, technologies, or practices, generating initial interest and creating a foundation for the innovation to build upon. Without them, innovations may struggle to gain the necessary traction.

3. **Trendsetters and Influencers:** Innovators and Early Adopters often serve as trendsetters and influencers within their respective communities or industries. Their adoption decisions can significantly impact the decisions of the Early Majority and even Late Majority. When the model downplays their role, it overlooks the ripple effect they create in driving adoption.

4. **Feedback and Improvement:** Innovators and Early Adopters are more likely to provide feedback, suggest improvements, and offer insights on

how to enhance the innovation. Their experiences can guide refinements that make the innovation more appealing to the later adopter categories. Neglecting their significance can lead to missed opportunities for innovation refinement.

5. **Champions of Change:** Early adopters are often passionate about the innovations they embrace. They can become champions for the innovation, actively promoting it and encouraging others to adopt it. By underemphasizing their importance, the model fails to acknowledge the critical role they play in the diffusion process.

6. **Risk-Taking Pioneers:** Innovators and Early Adopters are typically more willing to take risks and experiment with new ideas. Their willingness to adopt early can accelerate the innovation's path to the broader market. Without them, the innovation might face a slower and more challenging adoption journey.

7. **Complex Decision-Making:** The model simplifies the decision-making process by categorizing individuals into discrete groups. However, the reality is that adoption decisions are often more complex and influenced by a combination of individual characteristics and external factors. The model's focus on later adopter categories oversimplifies this complexity.

The Diffusion of Innovation model's primary emphasis on the later adopter categories can overshadow the pivotal roles played by Innovators and Early Adopters. To better understand and facilitate the adoption process, it's essential to recognize the unique contributions of these early adopter segments and their significance in driving innovation adoption and diffusion.

Examples:

1. **3D Printing:** In the realm of 3D printing, Innovators and Early Adopters played a crucial role in pushing the technology into various industries. They were the pioneers who recognized the potential of 3D printing for rapid prototyping, customized manufacturing, and even healthcare applications. Their early experiments and investments helped create a

broader market for 3D printing.

2. **Blockchain and Cryptocurrency:** The adoption of blockchain technology and cryptocurrencies like Bitcoin began with Innovators and Early Adopters. These tech enthusiasts and visionaries saw the disruptive potential of decentralized finance and blockchain applications. Their involvement and advocacy sparked interest among businesses and investors, eventually leading to wider adoption.

3. **Wearable Fitness Technology:** Innovators and Early Adopters were vital to the early success of wearable fitness technology, such as Fitbit and Apple Watch. They embraced these devices for tracking health and fitness metrics. Their positive experiences and recommendations influenced health-conscious individuals, leading to mainstream adoption.

4. **Plant-Based Foods:** The adoption of plant-based foods, particularly meat alternatives like Beyond Meat and Impossible Foods, was initially driven by Innovators and Early Adopters who sought more sustainable and ethical food options. Their support and feedback encouraged restaurants and retailers to offer plant-based products to a broader audience.

In conclusion, while the Diffusion of Innovation model offers valuable insights into the adoption and spread of new ideas, it has notable limitations. Understanding these limitations is essential for businesses and innovators seeking to navigate the complex landscape of innovation adoption effectively. By recognizing that adoption is not always a linear process and that various factors can lead to rapid or slowed adoption, stakeholders can adapt their strategies to better reflect the real-world dynamics of innovation diffusion.

* * *

4

Challenges of Group Brainstorming

It is a common misconception that group brainstorming sessions are the most effective way to generate ideas. Many people believe that bringing people together in an energetic and exciting atmosphere will lead to a greater number of ideas being produced. However, research has shown that this is not always the case.

 *"Group brainstorming sessions are like trying to juggle with one hand tied behind your back - it's entertaining, but you won't win any juggling contests."*

During my design college days and early in my working career, I took part in several group brainstorming sessions. Despite being interesting, fun, and energetic, I found that these sessions were not as productive as I had hoped in terms of generating good ideas.

Many organizations are increasingly relying on group brainstorming to increase creativity within the organization. However, while brainstorming is an effective method for generating new ideas and solving problems, group brainstorming may not always be as productive as individual brainstorming. There are several reasons for this, including production blocking, evaluation apprehension, and social loafing.

Production Blocking

Production blocking refers to the phenomenon where an individual's contribution to a task or discussion prevents others from participating. This can occur in group brainstorming sessions when one person is dominating the conversation, when one person's ideas are given more weight than others, or when individuals feel unable to speak up due to the group dynamic. This can have several negative consequences on the brainstorming process, such as delays in idea generation and articulation, making it difficult for other group members to contribute their ideas and preventing the emergence of new and diverse perspectives.

Furthermore, when individuals are monitoring and attending to others' speech and waiting for an opportunity to express their own ideas, it places additional cognitive load on the brain. This can prevent participants from generating additional ideas or refining existing ones, leading to a stagnation of ideas. The constant interruption of the train of thoughts also can cause the brainstorming sessions to become less productive.

To avoid production blocking, it is important to create an environment where all members feel comfortable expressing their ideas and where there are mechanisms in place to ensure that every member has the opportunity to contribute. This can include strategies such as having a designated facilitator who manages the flow of conversation, using round-robin brainstorming, where each member is given a set amount of time to share their ideas, and giving equal weight to all ideas, regardless of the source.

"Production blocking is like everyone trying to sing their solo in a choir concert at the same time. It's a beautiful mess, but let's not release this as an album."

Evaluation Apprehension

Evaluation apprehension is another potential cause of productivity loss in brainstorming groups. It refers to the fear of negative evaluation or rejection from other group members that can make individuals hesitant to express their views, ideas or opinions. This fear of judgment can lead to less participation and fewer ideas being shared in the group, which can limit the potential of the brainstorming sessions.

Individuals may be hesitant to express their ideas in a group setting due to concerns about being judged by others. This can be especially pronounced in situations where there are significant power imbalances or where individuals are not familiar with the other group members. These fears can manifest in various ways, including self-doubt, lack of self-confidence, and anxiety about how one's ideas will be received by others.

To overcome evaluation apprehension, it is important to create an environment that is safe and supportive for all members to express their ideas. This can include strategies such as:

- Establishing a set of ground rules that everyone agrees to, such as no negative criticism, and respecting everyone's ideas.
- Encouraging group members to share their ideas without fear of judgment.
- Making sure that everyone has equal opportunities to speak and express themselves.
- Having a designated facilitator who can help to manage the conversation and ensure that everyone's ideas are heard.
- Starting with low-stakes topics or task to warm up the group and build trust.

Creating a non-threatening and non-judgmental environment can help to reduce the fear of evaluation and increase participation, leading to a more productive brainstorming session and making sure that everyone's ideas are considered.

Social Loafing

Social loafing is the third problem that can arise during group brainstorming sessions, and it refers to the tendency of some individuals to not exert as much effort in team settings as when they are working alone. This happens when group size increases and individuals' contributions become less visible and it becomes more difficult to monitor individuals and hold them accountable for their participation, leading to decreased productivity.

As the group size increases, responsibility becomes diffused among a larger number of stakeholders, which makes it easier to engage in social loafing without the fear of activating self-sanctions. Furthermore, as the group size increases, the human aspect of group members becomes less salient, individuals in brainstorming teams might feel that they are interacting with a nameless crowd rather than individuals within a team. Such perceptions and feelings would deactivate the self-regulatory function because it fosters a perception of dissimilarity between the performer and the recipients.

To overcome social loafing, it is important to ensure that individuals are held accountable for their participation in the brainstorming session. This can include strategies such as:

- Breaking the group into smaller sub-groups
- Assigning specific roles and responsibilities to each group member
- Providing clear goals and expectations for participation
- Creating an environment where individuals are encouraged to take ownership of their ideas
- Having an independent third-party observer to monitor the participation and effort of each group member.

Additionally, fostering a sense of interdependence within the group by highlighting that success of the group project depends on everyone's effort could help to prevent social loafing, creating a sense of shared responsibility and encouraging individuals to pull their own weight.

Maximizing Group Brainstorming Effectiveness

To maximize the effectiveness of brainstorming sessions, it can be beneficial to first allow team members to generate ideas independently and then bring them together for a group discussion. This approach allows individuals to focus on their own ideas and think through them more thoroughly, without the pressure of a group setting. It also allows individuals to work at their own pace and generate a larger number of ideas.

After the individual brainstorming, the team should come together for a group discussion. During this discussion, each person can present their ideas and explain their thought process. This allows for the sharing of different perspectives and can lead to the emergence of new and diverse ideas. Team members can also gain insights from one another's ideas, and brainstorm on ways to combine or modify them.

After the group discussion, the team should be encouraged to generate another round of fresh ideas and refine some of their existing ones. By this point, team members will have subconsciously leveraged each other's creative thought processes, resulting in a greater number of higher quality ideas overall. By allowing for a round of individual brainstorming before and after the group discussion, individuals will have the opportunity to explore different directions peacefully and evaluate their own ideas, which is not possible in direct group brainstorming setting.

This approach of combining individual and group brainstorming can help to overcome the problems associated with group brainstorming and maximize the effectiveness of the brainstorming session, by leveraging the strengths of both individual and group brainstorming.

Conclusion

In conclusion, while group brainstorming can be a fun and interactive way to generate ideas, it can also come with its own set of challenges such as production blocking, evaluation apprehension, and social loafing. Combining the strengths of both individual and group brainstorming techniques can help organizations to overcome these challenges and maximize the productivity and creativity of brainstorming sessions. By encouraging individual brain-storming, creating a safe and supportive environment, holding individuals accountable and fostering a sense of interdependence within the group, organizations can improve the effectiveness of their brainstorming sessions.

* * *

About the Author

Shah Mohammed is an accomplished Business Strategy and design-thinking consultant with a passion for innovation and user-centred design. He is the founder of D-Cube Designs, a leading design consultancy based in Chennai, India. With a Master's degree in Design from IIT Kanpur, India, which he obtained in 2004, Shah brings a strong academic background and a wealth of practical experience to his work.

As an Industrial Designer, Shah has played a pivotal role in successfully developing and launching over 300 products across various industries over the past decade. His expertise spans the entire product lifecycle, from conducting in-depth user research to designing intuitive and aesthetically pleasing solutions. Shah's keen understanding of customer needs and his ability to translate them into innovative product designs have earned him a reputation for excellence in the industry.

In addition to his contributions to the field of design, Shah has also established himself as a sought-after Business Strategy consultant. Leveraging his customer-centric approach, he has provided valuable insights and guidance to businesses of all sizes, helping them identify market opportunities, develop effective strategies, and drive growth. His expertise in areas such as branding, emotional branding, creativity techniques, leadership, and building competitive advantages has made him a trusted advisor to CEOs, startup founders, and aspiring entrepreneurs.

Shah is an avid blogger and has been sharing his knowledge and insights through his blog for the past six years. With over three hundred articles covering a wide range of topics, including Branding lessons, Design Thinking, Business Strategy, and Psychology in Business, his blog has become a valuable resource for professionals seeking practical advice and inspiration. The lessons featured in this book are a curated selection of some of his most impactful blogs, offering readers timeless lessons and actionable strategies.

You can connect with me on:

- https://shahmm.medium.com
- https://twitter.com/shahbaba
- https://www.linkedin.com/in/shahmm

Also by Shah Mohammed

Books on Business Strategy and Leadership

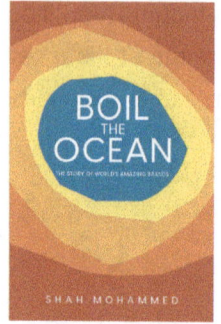

Boil The Ocean: The Story of World's Amazing Brands
Embark on a captivating journey through the world of iconic brands with "Boil The Ocean: The Story of World's Amazing Brands." This thought-provoking book offers a collection of insightful case studies that delve into the successes, failures, and transformative moments of some of the most renowned brands in history.

With meticulous research and captivating storytelling, "Boil The Ocean" offers valuable insights, timeless lessons, and inspiring narratives that will engage both business enthusiasts and casual readers. Whether you are an entrepreneur, marketer, designer, brand strategist, startup owner, CEO, brand consultant, or simply intrigued by the stories behind the brands we know and love, this book will leave you inspired, informed, and eager to explore the dynamic world of branding and business.

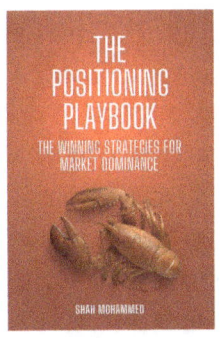

The Positioning Playbook: The Winning Strategies for Market Dominance

Unlock the secrets to market supremacy with "The Positioning Playbook: The Winning Strategies for Market Dominance." This comprehensive guide dives into the art and science of strategic positioning, revealing the proven strategies that will set your business apart from the competition and propel you to the top of your industry.

Discover the power of positioning, going beyond superficial branding and slogans, to create a deep and lasting impact on your target audience. Learn how to carve out a distinct space in consumers' minds, forging emotional connections and delivering unique value that resonates with their needs and desires.

Throughout the book, readers are introduced to thirteen effective positioning strategies, each serving as a pathway to achieving market dominance and sustainable success.

INCEPTION: Unveiling the Secrets of Inspirational Leadership

Unlock the secrets to becoming an exceptional leader with "Inception: Unveiling the Secrets of Inspirational Leadership." This captivating book takes you on a transformative journey, exploring the depths of leadership principles, personal development, strategic skills, decision-making, and cognitive biases that shape influential leaders.

Whether you are an aspiring leader seeking to develop your skills, an experienced executive striving for continuous growth, or someone passionate about unlocking the potential of inspirational leadership, this book is designed to provide you with valuable insights, practical strategies, and thought-provoking perspectives.

SUB-BRANDING PLAYBOOK: Winning Strategies for Targeted Growth

In this captivating playbook, you'll discover a treasure trove of sub-branding strategies, each chapter unveiling a different secret weapon to unlock targeted growth. From creating sub-brands for demographic segmentation to psychographic targeting and cultural branding, we leave no stone unturned.

The book provides insights into successful sub-branding initiatives through real-world case studies, offering practical, actionable strategies for leveraging sub-brands to achieve targeted growth. By examining the considerations and criteria for developing sub-brands, readers can understand how sub-brands contribute to brand differentiation, customer targeting, and market expansion.

Elevate your brand's position, attract a loyal customer base, and surpass your competition. The Sub-Branding Playbook is your trusted companion on this exciting adventure, offering guidance, inspiration, and a roadmap to targeted growth.

The Secret Strategies of Marketing: How Brands Use Cognitive Biases to Win Your Wallet

In a world bombarded by marketing messages, understanding the psychology that underpins consumer behaviour is the ultimate game-changer. Whether you're a marketer, entrepreneur, business owner, or an inquisitive consumer, this book unravels the mysteries behind why certain brands resonate deeply while others remain forgettable.

Your Guide to Cognitive Biases: This comprehensive guide explores a treasure trove of cognitive biases, from the well-known to the lesser-explored, offering profound insights into their applications and impact. From the allure of familiarity to the power of scarcity, you'll journey through a spectrum of biases that influence every purchase decision.

www.ingramcontent.com/pod-product-compliance
Lightning Source LLC
Chambersburg PA
CBHW072201290526
45794CB00004B/1596